M000196079

ENDORSEMENTS

"Cindy Paige takes a practical look at what steps to take on your journey with humor and realistic examples. 'IT' made me laugh out loud! This book gives you a guide to knowing where you want to go after a loss, and how you're going to get there."

Liam Stryder
Humorist

"Bravo for *Summit*! I love the analogy of facing our fears, our devastating moments, and our crises to climbing Mt. Everest. I appreciated how *Summit* pointed out that we can't just hope or wish our situation away – we have to plan, strategize, and face the things we fear the most. This book provides a wonderful guide/plan and laser focus tips and techniques to use when life throws us a curve ball. I am the mountain!"

Phyllis Flowers
Senior Manager, Learning &
Organizational Development

"As a therapist, what I was most struck by when working with Cindy on *Summit, A Guide from Pain to Peace,* was her encouraging, passionate "voice." It's as if she is ahead of us on the trail, saying, "C'mon - I know you can do it! I *know* you can move beyond this pain. I've done it, and I'll show you how." Cindy is an ever-present companion on the trek up the mountain to healing. And her insights and guidance for doing so are grounded in time-tested, effective strategies and spiritual faith. She illuminates moments when we can stop and consider how our actions may have contributed to painful pasts, as well as when we should rest and visualize our dreams for a peaceful, satisfying future. As her editor, I think that readers will especially appreciate the many vignettes illustrating challenges that most of us will face at some time in our lives. With this offering, Cindy has become one of the dependable sherpas to guide you through the most painful straits of your life. Good journey."

Tracy Hart,
LICSW/Editor

"As we all look for inspiration every day and certainly at this globally uncertain time with the pandemic looming over all our lives, now more than ever, the insights of Cindy Paige are priceless in her book, *Summit.* Cindy brings us into her well-earned experiences and wisdom with a gentle humility to engage the reader to see themselves in each scenario of the metaphor of the summit. We all find insurmountable mountains of challenges in our lives, as well as, the many valleys. Cindy takes us through the way to evaluate and discern the best goal to set, to strategically plan the course, how to pivot and course correct to both survive and thrive and then the achievement and road back to reflect and celebrate a win and plan for the next. This book is for anyone simply looking for inspiration or for someone seeking a much more intrinsic meaning to deepen your personal awareness to navigate your external and internal emotional world. Cindy's *Summit* is a must read during this most prescient time of global and personal transformation."

Fara Gold McLaughlin
Founder & CEO
GoldMark Seniors
Specializing in Senior Housing Strategic Marketing and Management Services

SUMMIT

A Guide from Pain to Peace

CINDY PAIGE

AUTHOR ACADEMY elite

Published by Author Academy Elite
PO Box 43, Powell, OH 43065
www.AuthorAcademyElite.com

Identifiers:
Library of Congress Control Number: 2020909458
ISBN: 978-1-64746-293-2 (paperback)
ISBN: 978-1-64746-294-9 (hardback)
ISBN: 978-1-64746-295-6 (ebook)

Available in paperback, hardback, e-book, and audiobook

All Scripture quotations, unless otherwise indicated, are taken from the Holy Bible, New International Version®, NIV®. Copyright © 1973, 1978, 1984 by Biblica, Inc.™ Used by permission of Zondervan. All rights reserved worldwide.

Any Internet addresses (websites, blogs, etc.) and telephone numbers printed in this book are offered as a resource. They are not intended in any way to be or imply an endorsement by Author Academy Elite, nor does Author Academy Elite vouch for the content of these sites and numbers for the life of this book.

Some names and identifying details have been changed to protect the privacy of individuals.

Dedication

This book is dedicated to my husband, Curtis. You are my best friend, my partner, and my love. Thank you for your unwavering support, my Sirdar, my chief Sherpa. There would be no summit without you.

...and to the many other Sherpas in my life - past, present and future.

USE THIS BOOK TO HELP NAVIGATE BEYOND THE PAIN CAUSED BY THESE (AND OTHER) STORMS:

Death...of a child, partner, parent, sibling, or close friend
A loved one's suicide
Loss of fidelity
Divorce
Loss of custody
Disease
Gradual loss of a loved one due to Alzheimer's or dementia
Abuse: sexual, physical, or emotional
Loss during childhood
Survivor guilt
Loss of job
Empty nest syndrome
Loss of life as you expected
Your personal storm

TABLE OF CONTENTS

Thank you for letting me join you on your journey. If you are 'Summit Bound' and would like to climb deeper into some of the tips and tools introduced in *Summit*, visit my website at www.cindypaige.org.

THE STORM

The storm screams. Wind-whipped snow densely blankets me
Visibility is nil, and gusts of wind beat me from all directions
A whiteout
My chest is heavy, but not with the effort of exertion
Something bigger
What is happening? Something is wrong
Cold sinks into me like death
Why is everything white?
And why is it so cold?
Reality harshly soaks in; I close my eyes
Despair washes through me, colder than the freezing air
I hope this is a dream
Pray it is
But there is nothing dreamlike about the storm that rages
Snow so thick I can't tell if the road is in front of, or behind me
Where am I?
I bury my face beneath my hands, teeth clench, a barrier against
tears scalding the back of my eyes
I will not cry. I've cried enough for a lifetime. Two lifetimes
A whiteout
If only…
What I wouldn't give to be one of these nameless snowflakes.
To drift out of the sky, not caring where I land, lasting only a
heartbeat before dissolving into nothingness. One frozen moment
of existence, one easy freefall

Done
Gone
Over
Anything would be better than this terrifying silence
Even the silence is muffled
I look at the snow-covered ground, wishing I could just lie down
... let the cold seep in and coax me into a forever sleep. Is it the
fog in my mind, or is there fog around me, too? I realize my breath
is making crystalline clouds in the icy air—tiny puffs that appear
and drift, dissipate and disappear. I stare at the misty evidence
of my existence and know what it is to be truly afraid
And I know how hard it is going to be to conquer this fear
Until then, I will do what I do best
Survive

INTRODUCTION

This book focuses on a journey that we shall all travel at some point in our lives. It's the route out of pain and loss. I liken tragedy to a devastating blizzard. While the storm rages on, you are terrified. The wind, the snow, the formidable sounds of fierce weather surround you. You prepare, search for resources, fight—try to get through each day and survive. The future, or what you'll be left with when the blizzard is over, is unknown.

Our storms hit in a variety of forms—each as individual as we are. Some are predicted, slow to build, then last so long we give up hope that we'll escape. Others can arise with dazzling suddenness, seemingly out of nothing, leaving devastation and destruction in their wake. Cold, deep, and universal (yet as unique as a single snowflake), feelings which follow the tempest make themselves known. The worst may have passed or more devastation of life as we know it is on its way. The only thing we can be certain of—we are in terrible pain.

The divorce is final.

A family member's battle with cancer has ended.

Wounds took your leg.

Our home is gone.

A beloved child died by suicide.

You are in survival mode. It was a cataclysmic storm, but you knew you had to get through it. Now the worst of it has settled, and you realize you are lost. Left with heartache. He'll never walk through that door again. There will never be another Christmas at Grandma's house. You'll never walk again. The unimaginable has happened, but you must go on.

This book's aim is to help you do that and support you along the way. We'll start right now: I want to suggest something for you to try. I know it will be difficult, but for a moment…think forward. Imagine what it might be like once you're through this painful time. At the moment, it may not seem possible that holding onto life will ever feel comfortable again, that you will laugh spontaneously, or find joy in the people or events around you. But you will. The sun will rise and eventually shine after a storm. So, take a slow, deep breath. Can you create in your mind what the return of "fair weather" could look like? Where are you? Who is with you? How are you feeling? What are you doing? Wherever or whatever that is, that is your summit—if you can climb out of this anguish, you will get there. And that's where you'll find peace.

I was at this crucial crossroad in my own life when I had a dream. It was like no other I can remember. I was lost in a violent blizzard. Trying to get somewhere; but I had no idea where or which way to go or what I needed to do to get there. As the worst of the storm moved on, I was alone in waist-high snow, aimlessly wading through it. But it came to me: If I could just make it through this snow, I would be okay. The snow became less deep, but travel was uphill. If I could just make it up this hill, I would find my way. A sudden and desperate longing came over me. If I could just keep climbing, I would find my way. I could reach my summit.

Loss visits all of us. The funeral is over, and everyone has gone home. Now what do you do? The kids are at your ex's, and you are utterly alone in a house built to be filled with family. Now what do you do? Rehab is over, and you are on your own. Now what do you do? *Summit* is a collection of stories, thoughts and ideas, woven into a metaphor of climbing a mountain. It is meant to inspire and strengthen you, wherever you might be in this process. It's filled with tips and suggestions for how to continue to climb and navigate the various aspects of your personal journey. Though our stories may differ, the destination is the same for everyone: to reach our summit. Peace from the pain we are feeling. Peace in the new life we are challenged to create. Peace we can enjoy. Peace we can celebrate. Peace and happiness.

THE SUN

A bright sun shines through the ice crystals
Everything sparkles

But not with beauty
Too dead and austere for beauty
Everything has shifted; nothing is the same
Ahead lies my new path, my 'mountain'
Depressingly steep and formidable
I feel suspended in slow motion
I can't move
I won't move
I might not ever move, except

Except

Except for that most basic human instinct
The instinct to survive

THE STORM

In life, there is no shortage of storms. Situations that are "not fair." Sequences of pain and loss shock us, test us, and leave us wondering how we'll go on. We wonder if there's any guiding hand whatsoever in the universe. Survivors have to push forward, focusing upon what we *can* control, to arrive at a place of peace and acceptance. Our difficulties teach us we're not in control, at least not completely, and the manner in which we've handled our lives so far may not serve us well going forward. There are lessons to be learned, heartaches to endure, and a grappling acceptance of our new life situation. Crises force us to stretch in completely unfamiliar ways; but first we have to survive the here and now. We can't stay at this crossroads of darkness and desperation. Where to begin?

THE SUN

Believe in yourself. The sun shines after a storm. We must find what will make us shine in the aftermath of the storm. Ask yourself: Who am I? Who will I become as a survivor? We can get mired down in the depths of our own despair. Questioning: Can we succeed in this new role? The first and most immediate step in survival mode is to gather our inner gear and believe that we do, indeed, have what it takes to climb this mountain.

Whisper it or shout it out: **I Will Survive!**

In times of sorrow, it's easy to get swamped by a deluge of self-doubt, failures, and things we don't like about ourselves. We feel crushed. In pain. Exhausted, physically and emotionally. And who knows our faults and shortcomings better than us? Tune in to your inner voice. How are you speaking to yourself? Do you find yourself thinking:

- This is my fault.

- I can't do this.

- I am worthless.

- I'll never succeed.

- I deserve this.

- I can't support my family.

- I'm too fat and ugly to be loved.

- Even God doesn't love me.

To become aware of our own negative self-concepts is the first priority. We have to prepare for this trek into survival. This step is like checking that our backpack of provisions doesn't include an extra 10-pound weight.

After a crisis which has changed our lives, it's natural to second-guess ourselves and our decisions. This is especially true if others have been affected and are hurting too. Maybe we are being blamed for their pain and wonder if there's any truth to that. Thoughtfully reflecting on events may help us to stand by our choices.

Tough Call
My mother served as the Power of Attorney for her aunt. At 98, Great Aunt Marcella was declining and rushed to the hospital after a fall. She was admitted that final time with weight loss, dehydration, and congestive heart failure. Marcella couldn't (or wouldn't) eat and could barely drink. Decisions had to be made. This type of drama far exceeded what my mother was emotionally equipped to deal with, so I was left in charge. I dug in. I found babysitters for my kids, stayed with her every day in the hospital and consulted with her doctors. The only option to sustain life at this point was a feeding tube. Many in the family and her circle of friends wanted this to happen. I began to research. I met with her priest and again with her doctor. What would it be like for her to endure the procedure and then live with a feeding tube? The decision was made; it was challenged, and then there was blame.

It's easy to let self-doubt creep in, holding you hostage for your actions, especially during tough times. When there's conflict, self-doubt can send you spiraling into despair, but ask yourself—did I do the best I could do at that moment with the information I had at that point in time? If your answer is yes, take heart. Faith was the most important aspect of my Great Aunt Marcella's life, and I followed, with faith, the guidelines from her church, the doctors, and what we believed to be the right course of action for her. I consulted with my mom and sister on decisions made, but when challenges came, I was able to shield my mom from hurtful accusations. I felt confident that as difficult as they were, the right decisions had been made. We lost our beloved aunt, but she didn't suffer unduly. I was hurting, and I was challenged, but when it got ugly, I could still believe in myself.

TAKE FOUR

Four steps to believing in yourself:

1. **Change your focus to empower *you*.** Think, "*When* I get through this…," not "*If* I get through this." Where are opportunities for growth, love, fulfillment? Only *you* have the power to get you where you want to be. At any given moment, you have the authority to say, "This is *not* how my story is going to end."

2. **Recognize your potential.** Although human, full of flaws and failings, each of us has another side of our humanity: an enormous potential within that we rarely acknowledge. In a journal or on a piece of paper, answer these questions:

   "What do I like about myself?"
   "What am I good at?"
   "What have I done that I should feel proud of?"

If it's difficult to get in touch with positives, know that friends or loving family members often see things about us that we are blind to. Ask yourself, "What might *others* say are my strengths?" "What do *others* appreciate about me?" Don't be afraid to ask them directly, they might surprise you.

To counter the energy-draining, negative inner voice and to develop a supportive self-image, we must force ourselves to cognitively intervene. Note the old self-talk, but challenge it with thoughts on a higher plane of optimism and potential. Push yourself a little bit outside your comfort zone of believing the old, false ideas about yourself to tap into the possibility of inner awesomeness. This is tough. You are hurting and overwhelmed—but do what you can and keep coming back

> "THEY DID NOT KNOW THEIR LIMITATIONS, AND THEREFORE HAD NONE."
> UNKNOWN

to this. Start a list of ways you shine. It may start with only one thing, but as time goes by, adding to it will grow a more clear, positive way of feeling about yourself and your potential.

The Elephant Rope (origin unknown)
As a man was passing the elephants, he suddenly stopped, confused by the fact that these huge creatures were being held by only a small rope tied to their front leg. No chains, no cages. It was obvious that the elephants could, at any time, break away from their bonds but for some reason, they did not. He saw a trainer nearby and asked why these animals just stood there and made no attempt to get away. "Well," the trainer said, "when they were very young and much smaller, we used the same sized rope to tie them. At that age, it's enough to hold them. As they grow up, they are conditioned to believe they cannot break away. They believe the rope can still hold them, so they never try to break free." The man was amazed. These animals could at any time break free from their bonds but because they believed they couldn't, they were stuck right where they were.

Like the elephants, how many of us go through life conditioned to believe that we cannot do something, simply because we failed at it once before? Failure is part of learning—this knowledge actually increases the possibility for future success! (If we aren't defensive and view the event with a bit of emotional distance.) Break out of the mindset that failure is bad and pain is a dirty secret. Don't listen to the strongholds placed *on you*, or *by you*, which you carry from your childhood. Take stock of the depth of your potential. Believe in yourself—in your power!

3. **Neutralize Fear**. Fear, by definition, is the expectation of pain. Some fears are instinctual, like fear of physical harm or the fear of falling. Other fears are learned: fear of failure, fear of rejection, fear of consequences, fear of the future. Fear is also a natural reaction to *change*. One strategy for managing *this* fear is to take control of as many of the puzzle pieces of your life as possible. Start by naming the fear. What are you most afraid of? Being alone? Living without them? Handling the financial consequences of this crisis? Having support or feeling isolated? Holidays? Not knowing how long until you feel like yourself again? There is no benefit in fearing what you have no control over. If a problem is fixable—if the fear is such that you can do something to solve it, then make a plan. If not, let it go. Live in today, not borrowing fear for what might happen tomorrow.

Shed a Little Light
Bobby was afraid of the dark. His fear kept him from joining other boys for sleepovers, but this was his best friend Leo's birthday, so he decided to give it a try. As the boys settled down in their sleeping bags in front of the TV, Bobby held tight to the flashlight his dad had given him. Just as he was falling asleep, he saw a movement.

*Was it a monster? A crazy escaped convict who tortured little boys? He pulled out his flashlight and aimed it toward the kitchen. Oh, the monster was only Leo's mom, putting out donuts for hungry boys who might wake up early. We never let our imagination run away with the **good** things that could happen. With a little light, maybe we can find more donuts in the morning.*

Shining a light on our fears signals, to ourselves, that we are ready to courageously deal with the storm. That we are willing to:

> 4. **Take Action**. Actions reflect beliefs. By taking even the smallest steps, we communicate to our self and the world: I believe in myself and my journey. Staying passive fuels depression, while taking action raises self-esteem and generates feelings of power and hope. Be as consistent as possible. Do at least one thing every day to move through the pain. Show *yourself* that you believe! You are reading this book. That's action! Take a shower. Get dressed. Go for a walk.

So Where Is Your Starting Point?

Whatever the nature of your storm—you are hurting. Before you can begin to move forward on your journey, you have to address where you are. Even your car's GPS (global positioning system) makes you identify your current location. Your starting point…is your pain.

"Ugh. No! I'm barely 'believing in myself' and getting dressed every day. The pain is what I'm hiding from. As long as I don't 'go *there*,' I can survive. How about some tips on *that*?!"

You're right. This is normally what we don't want to do. It goes against a basic human instinct—to protect. Avoid, repress, deny. Numb, hide, eat, disengage—all ways we self-protect.

And unfortunately, we live in a culture that supports self-destructive coping mechanisms. When a storm hits, we usually try to take control of things and solve them, forget them or deny them—instead of accept them, experience them, or try to see the meaning they may hold for us. Who hasn't heard:

Move on!
Chin up.
Keep busy.
You're better off.
They're in a better place.

But you can't chart your course without knowing where you start. As much as you don't like it, acknowledge what you are going through. There is a new normal to accept. Own what has happened, and rally your strength to deal with it. Moving through and beyond pain is a process. And right now, you are grieving the loss of whatever your storm has damaged. A lost loved one, the relationship you thought would last, the career you were so sure of, the healthy body you took for granted...

Respect your need to grieve, to mourn, to shed your tears. You have to recognize and allow yourself to be in the grieving process. A wise counselor of mine once said, "Why do you think you shouldn't be sad?" Give yourself permission to feel what you feel. Don't let sadness consume you, but allow yourself space to feel the pain. In doing so, you create a foundation for the healing process. And healing is the gift we give ourselves when we acknowledge our brokenness. You can't go back and change the beginning, but you can start where you are and change the ending.

GOOD GRIEF!

Grief is good. It's a natural reaction to the loss of loving someone, or something, very dear to us. It's normal, and it's necessary. It's been said that grief is the emotion we fear the most. Amen to that! We avoid it and steer clear of anyone who appears to be in the throes of it. Have you been to a funeral recently? Anyone caught crying is often isolated from the crowd. You may think you are giving them privacy during their time of pain. Are you? Or are you staying as far away from that exposed grief as possible? What if it's contagious? It makes me so uncomfortable. Oh no. No! No. No. No. I don't want to get near pain like that. Funerals today have become more like parties, a celebration of the life that has ended. There is certainly a need for shared memories of happy times—but not to the exclusion of denying the pain of the loss.

Grief is the aftermath left in the trail of the storm, and it has to be dealt with. Locking up sadness and pain and pretending that they aren't there, causes poison in an already painful wound. It may work for a while, but eventually our feelings will demand expression. Which is necessary, because you need an intimate understanding of your emotions in the aftermath of the storm. If you want to heal from it, you have to go through it; you cannot go around it. And, it cannot be rushed. Time alone does not bring healing for grief. It's what you do *with* the time that makes the difference.

> "THE ONLY FEELINGS THAT DO NOT HEAL ARE THE ONES YOU HIDE."
> HENRI NOUWEN

After reading countless theories, stages and thoughts on grieving, I've gathered them together into what I call **The Four Ps**. Can you identify where you are in the grief process?

- **Protect.** Your first response to pain is to protect yourself. To avoid the pain and the feelings that come with it. Sometimes this shows up as denial. It is a natural defense mechanism that kicks in as you are forced to accept the unthinkable. Denial can sometimes help us to absorb tragic news at a slower rate so we are not completely overwhelmed by it.

- **Prevent.** What could I have done to prevent this? "What if...?" "If only I'd..." Anger, resentment, bargaining. Take some time to sort out the true scope of your responsibility or control. We can't control what we have no control over, but that doesn't stop us from wishing we could have changed the path to destruction we are facing. If not resolved, intense feelings of guilt or remorse can block the healing process. This can lead to serious depression or unhealthy coping mechanisms.

- **Pout.** Be sad!! Wallow in it. This sucks! You have every right to feel unhappy and depressed, though it's a scary part of grieving. We have to allow ourselves time to be sad, and possibly to disengage from our regular routines. But recognize when you may have crossed into an unhealthy phase of depression. Not eating, sleeping, or showering, are flags to seek professional help. It's not shameful; it's smart. You are in the middle of a mess of devastation without the right tools to handle it. You wouldn't try to clean up tornado wreckage with a fork. For goodness sake, go buy a shovel!

- **Persevere.** Your loss eventually becomes integrated into your life story. You go on. Life goes on.

Grief is a reminder of the depth of our love. The Four Ps are reflective of my own journey. I remember learning the five stages of grief in a college psychology class: Denial, Anger, Bargaining, Depression, and Acceptance, by Elizabeth Kubler-Ross. She wrote the definitive work about grief in her 1969 book, *On Death and Dying*. Since then, there have been many attacks on her work, different theories, deeper interpretations of each stage. But I am struck most by how she's responded to misunderstandings about her contribution to the research. In her book with David Kessler, *On Grief and Grieving: Finding the Meaning of Grief Through the Five Stages of Loss*, she said, "They (the five stages of grief) were never meant to tuck messy emotions into neat packages. They are responses to loss that many people have, but there is not a typical response to loss, as there is no typical loss." She feels these stages are tools to help us frame and identify what we may be feeling as a result of various losses in our lives.

Alleluia! Grieving is a complex process. And it's messy! There are NO hard and fast rules, no timeline. Each and every one of us is unique. Recognize that! Check out where you are. Get help if you need it.

STOP CRYING!

Why? Why are we plagued with so many barriers to showing our emotions? Tears are a natural and appropriate expression of the pain associated with loss. Tears are the medicine of grieving. When you cry, your loss moves through you to the point of exit. That which is eating you up, as you try to hold it inside, gets released, and you can move on. Crying releases harmful negative chemicals that build up in your body due to stress. Let it out. If you need to cry, have at it. If not, that's ok too. Be yourself. Know what you feel and what you need. What's important is to do what is intuitively YOU. Forcing yourself to not cry, or to cry, or excessive crying—can be more harmful than good.

The British are Coming.
I'm a Crier! Yep! I cry. Loud, and often. Normal and acceptable, yes. But let's be honest, you can't cry all of the time. In front of your young children. In line at the grocery store. In a meeting at work. It scares people. But I teeter on the brink of excessive

crying—so I took some good advice. Make an appointment with yourself to grieve. I would try to control my emotions in public or in front of the kids. But when I was alone, or with a trusted friend, I would allow myself to think about the storm, the pain, the fear, and I could cry. Allowing myself to naturally express my pain helped me to move through it.

No matter which storm has raged through your life, it's okay to admit you feel angry, upset, fearful, and vengeful.

- Set aside 15 minutes each day to feel your emotions. Allow yourself the same compassion you would grant another person you love. Do not judge yourself. Don't let your mind interfere; simply sit and feel what you feel.

- You can journal your thoughts and feelings.

- Don't be afraid to cry if you need to.

Your life only gets better when you do. Work on yourself, and the rest will follow.

MEN ARE DIFFERENT

Different how? Compared to women? Isn't that stating the obvious? You would think so, but it does bear further explanation. When it comes to 'feelings,' men and women's are distinctive. Our brains are wired differently, our hormones and emotional needs are not the same.

Women are prone to talk about what they are thinking and feeling. They communicate their emotional states with tears, facial expressions, hand gestures, and body language. Many women seem to be more comfortable figuring out how they feel by talking through it.

Men tend to work out their emotions by finding solutions and action. Most men want to manage things and maintain control. Often, a man will avoid highly emotionally charged settings when he hasn't got a plan. (Know any men who habitually avoid conflict or "discussion" of difficult issues?) Unfortunately, due to cultural pressure, men often stuff uncomfortable feelings (sadness, vulnerability, envy), letting them simmer and brew, and potentially eat away at them. Eventually, they may become twisted into anger or violence. They probably *are* as emotional as women, but don't appear so when their feelings are suppressed. It's not a matter of having the feelings, but more about how they process those emotions.

Regardless of one's gender, life is not 'tidy or nice,' and pretending it is or keeping one's emotions bottled up, will only hinder your own healing and journey through pain.

Buried Truth
Life had been good to Mark, with a successful career, loving wife, healthy children, and a nice home. He had it all, and he was in the driver's seat of his picture-perfect life. But, life's not without its challenges, and with a growing family, career, bills, responsibilities, and obligations, Mark became overwhelmed. He was losing control. When his marriage began to crumble, he desperately tried to force his wife, children, and LIFE, back within the boundaries that he understood and could command. His idyllic world fell apart. To resolve his feelings of loss and failure, he rewrote—in his mind—truths he could accept. He hadn't failed, his wife had. He hadn't loved her anyway. He hadn't lost the big sale at work. The client was a jerk. He hadn't been too drunk to drive; he was just blowing off steam. He hadn't cheated on his wife. That woman was only a friend. Initially that mental strategy worked, but eventually he was caught up in a web of untruths and rewritten history which conflicted with what others knew or remembered. He had put himself into a vicious cycle of

trying to maintain power over situations and emotions that he could not control.

Hurt doesn't go away simply because we refuse to acknowledge it. It's tempting to think that denying pain or painful truths will keep them from being true. Ultimately, avoidance takes over our lives. Not owning and integrating our stories affects our emotional health and physical well-being.

Prepare Your Body and Your Mind

Shape Up!

Although we are not literally training for a mountain trek to an actual summit, it would be remiss to think that physical fitness and health do not play a significant role in our overall journey. It's the difference between having stamina to support our efforts, or letting low energy or illness drain us when we need to feel strong.

Feeling even mildly depressed can prompt high-calorie comfort eating, or make the idea of exercising totally unappealing. Finding a friend to schedule regular brisk walks or to join you at the gym can serve three purposes: eliminate feelings of isolation, build vitality, and provide an emotional boost from endorphins. Try to eat right (more veggies), drink more water, stay active, and get some sleep. Fuel your physical health to support your emotional strength!

Change your Perspective

For every storm in life, there are various angles from which to view it. Much of your success in reaching the summit will involve your ability to reframe your situation. Auschwitz survivor, Viktor Frankl, said that our chosen response to life is our final and ultimate freedom. Our perspective literally has the power to keep us alive or cause our death. In his book, *Man's Search for Meaning*, Frankl insists that we must learn to see life as meaningful despite our circumstances. He emphasizes that there is an ultimate purpose to life. We cannot avoid suffering, but we can choose how to cope with it, find meaning in it, and move forward.

Much of our unhappiness comes from our reactions and perceptions to events in our lives. Learning to avoid destructive emotions and develop positive ones is an ongoing process. This takes time and practice. However, changing our perspective is much easier than changing our emotions. Maybe we will gag if someone tells us to look for the silver lining. Maybe we aren't ready to reframe pain this great, that could only be the result of an initial gift of a deep and unconditional love. But at some point, focus not on the loss, but on the gift of having loved.

> "TIS BETTER TO HAVE LOVED AND LOST, THAN NEVER TO HAVE LOVED AT ALL."
> ALFRED LORD TENNYSON

Remind yourself of how strong and resilient you have been during other tough times. How did you persevere? How did you grow? Could this be an opportunity to learn, to develop, or simply to embrace a new avenue previously closed off? When you look at things from this perspective, it can feel empowering. And remember! Just because an event unfolded in a particular way, doesn't mean it will happen again. Even patterns and habits can be altered and broken with awareness and effort!

Aesop's The Lion and the Statue
A man and a lion were discussing the relative strength of men and lions in general. The man contended that he and his fellows were stronger than lions by reason of their greater intelligence. "Come now with me," he cried, "and I will soon prove that I am right."

So he took the lion into the public gardens and showed him a statue of Hercules overcoming the lion and tearing his mouth in two. "That is all very well," said the lion, "but proves nothing, for it was a man who made the statue."

It's a matter of perspective. We can easily represent things as we wish them to be. Challenge yourself to consider another point of view.

FACE YOUR REALITY GAP

Life's not fair. And, it's not what you see on TV—even when it's labeled 'reality TV'. Often life offers one option when you want an entirely different one. The greater the distance between what you have and what you want, the greater the pain you may experience. Fighting reality is wasting energy. Recognize that the reality you wanted did not come true, and you must shift to living in a different world. Instead of resenting your situation, acknowledge that you must adapt.

For instance, if you lack financial resources, don't keep spending money like you have it. Acknowledge that your financial habits are out of line, and get started on a plan to change them. If you thought that when you got married, your wife would stay home, raise the children, and keep the house clean—wake up. She's at work, and you are going to have to vacuum. If you thought a college degree was your ticket to a six-figure salary and no one's called you with an offer, you might have to work in retail a little longer. You might have to be patient until economic factors change. You were sure that you and the love of your life would grow old together. Now, you're not. This isn't a negative message on squashing your dreams—but a reality check. Be realistic about where you are at this moment, in this situation.

Mom's Doing Great
Bryan saw his mom and dad regularly. Mike and Rachel lived nearby, and he often stopped after work to talk with his dad or drop off food from his wife. Sometimes they came to his house for dinner. Everyone knew that when Grandma started a story, she would likely repeat one or many parts several times, get flustered, and give up. No one paid much attention, and Bryan enjoyed talking 'shop' with his dad. It was a shock when Mike got the virus—and never recovered.

Rachel went on living in the house she and her husband had shared over the last forty years, and Bryan got caught up in his work, family, and grieving the loss of his dad. He called Rachel every weekend, and she seemed fine and busy, never talking for long. But the next time he stopped in with some leftover cake, Bryan couldn't believe what he found: dishes piled in the sink, his mom disheveled and dirty, wearing clothes that looked like they hadn't been washed for weeks. There were pills spilled on the kitchen table and spoiled milk in the refrigerator. Something was desperately wrong.

What Bryan learned was that while he had thought everything was fine with Rachel, the reality was that she had been steadily declining with dementia for years. Mike had been physically taking care of her and their home almost single handedly as her ability to perform tasks became more limited. It was a shock, but Bryan accepted that Rachel needed help. He'd need to grieve the loss of his father while taking over the care of his mother.

SHIFT INTO THE PRESENT

When the storm raged around you, your survival mission was clear. Your goal was compelling. Your focus laser-like. Your power reserves of energy, determination and courage were tapped. But when the storm subsides...

Treating the Cancer
Li's husband Simon was diagnosed with stage four liver cancer.
Devastating and painful, but only the beginning of hardship to
come. Years were spent in treatment, research, and the physical
fight to survive. The mission was to fight the cancer and cure
Simon. When he lost his battle, the storm died too. The clear
sense of purpose Li had during the storm enabled her to focus all
efforts on what mattered most, compelling them to take risks and
push forward, regardless of the odds or obstacles. But, now that
the storm was over, her purpose had shifted. To what?

Without purpose, we can fall into disillusionment, distraction, and despair. What is your reason for moving forward? Knowing what you want is good, but digging into why you want it will help propel you out of the mire and onto the road to recovery.

What vision or passion compels you to want to move forward? Passion is energy. Feel the power that comes from focusing on what excites you. Do you have children to raise and support? Young or old, are they watching to see how you model handling loss and change? Wouldn't the person no longer in your life want you to be as strong and loving as before? What are your priorities? Why? Our why and our dreams tangle together to become our summit.

Your Why? Why, by definition, means 'for what cause, reason, or purpose?' Humans need more than to simply survive. Understanding your *why* is a first, real step in figuring our your *how*. A clear sense of purpose can help you tap into knowledge and energy you didn't realize you had. With your *why* incorporated in your summit, you will find the courage to take the risks needed to get moving, stay motivated when challenged with obstacles. and move your life onto an entirely new and rewarding trajectory. Your talents, your values, your passions, and your skills, support your *why*, but how do you begin to find it?

- Create a vision board. This was a simple bulletin board in my bedroom. I didn't realize at the time that it was my vision board. It's where I showcased things that made me smile. The worn friendship bracelet my daughter made for me that summer; a note from my son; a magazine clipping of a happy-looking, retired couple; a scripture; a name badge from my job… A story emerged. A pattern. I learned a lot about my soul's desires by studying that bulletin board.

- Don't give up your hobbies. What inspires you or excites you can sometimes reveal a direction to travel: a stimulating career in a field you are passionate about; new friends with similar interests.

- Notice what you notice. What do you 'like' on social media? What do you post about? What gets your attention? The topics that get you talking or drive your interest are the ones that you care a great deal about.

- Research. Careers, housing, education, child-rearing. You don't know what you don't know—so read, listen and learn.

- Keep talking. Put your phone down and talk. Talk to your neighbors, talk to the person in line with you at the coffee shop, other people at the same conference, or in the waiting room at the pediatrician's office. Connections, ideas, and opportunities are everywhere, if we speak up and listen.

Now You're Talking
Keisha was chatting with one of the vendors at her daughter's
school fund-raiser. Since Vince got laid off, money was tight, so
she was making up for not buying anything by complimenting
the woman's sweater. The woman told her that she got it at a
shop at the mall where she worked weekends, and that they were
looking for more help. Keisha was surprised by the hourly wage
and the hours. Wow, that schedule would work around the kids
and maybe it would be enough to make sure the mortgage got
paid until Vince found something else. It turns out, Keisha liked
working outside her home. She had pride in contributing to the
financial well-being of her family and felt more confident. Vince
felt less pressure and stress in his new job, knowing he and Keisha
were a team. Several things shifted in Vince and Keisha's vision
for future dreams, as a result of one simple conversation.

VISION CHECK

You are already equipped with some important tools for your
journey. Compass points, if you will, of foresight, hindsight,
and insight. Turning the lens of your life into focus can help
you with your map. This is a prime example of a time to get
your pen out and try your hand at journaling.

Foresight. Can foresight be 20/20? How close can we get?
Look forward. What could manifest in your future? Don't let
your current reality hold you down. If life were perfect and
things came easily, where would you want to be? What would
you be doing? Dream. Think. Pray. Make a list. More than a
bucket list. Be bold. Be fearless!

Hindsight. It is said that we learn from history or are
doomed to repeat it. Think about past experiences. Where
have you been? What have you learned? What mistakes have
you made? What successes can you celebrate? What patterns
do you repeat? What were your expectations? Hindsight is the
tendency for people to view events as more predictable than

they actually were. Visualize a file in your head marked 'expectations.' Whenever you start dwelling on how things should be or should have been, mentally store the thought in this file. Expectations can be dangerous. They are rarely lived up to and even more rarely communicated to those closest to us.

Insight. Look within. What do you really want? Not what you think you are supposed to do, want, or be. But, what do *you* want? What will feel satisfying? Stimulating? How could you use and develop a hinted at interest, known talent, or hidden passion?

So, right about now you may be thinking: How great that I found this book. You feel bad. Really bad. However! You believe in yourself enough to acknowledge how much pain you are in and how bad you feel. Are we going anywhere with this? Hang on! That's exactly what we are doing. Going somewhere.

THE MAP

Survival!
Survival!
I need to take action
But what?
My skin is crawling with anxiety
It's cold and getting colder
The nameless dark enshrouds me
Stark
Grey
Raw
Where is color, movement?
I see boulders, I see snow
I could curl up among the rocks and drifts of snow
Give in to the mindless bliss of exhaustion
Minutes tick the silence into hours
Defeat
Give up?
No
I won't give in
Move
Move forward
Dear God! I don't want to
Resolve
One tiny, shuffling footstep at a time
Breathe

One ice cold, knife-sharp breath at a time
In. Out
Step. Step
In. Out
Step. Step
I see nothing
In. Out
Step. Falter
I stumble in the frozen tundra and land on my hands
The ice grates across my palm
The sharp sting of tearing flesh brings a new source of pain
I live, I feel, I hurt
I look down at the snow and the offending ice beneath it
I see something other than white
Ice
Rock
It's some sort of path

DISCOVER YOUR ROUTE AND CLIMB!

If this is a climb out of pain and devastation, you probably feel like you are at the base of Mount Everest. As the most famous mountain in the world, even the least adventurous of us has heard of Everest. Reaching 29,029 feet (8,848 meters), above sea level, it is the tallest mountain on Earth. To put that into perspective, it is roughly as tall as cruising altitude for an airplane! The average expedition to climb to the top of the world's highest peak takes almost two months.

Doesn't that climb seem unimaginable? Impossible? Certain death? Yet this metaphor is not meant to discourage your taking on a challenge difficult to complete, but to expose the parallels in achieving your own greatest climb. During raw, formidable life phases, it's hard to look forward, and it's painful to look back. But like a master mountaineer or an unseasoned climber who enlists an experienced Sherpa guide, you need a plan—some semblance of control, in an otherwise uncontrollable situation.

If this were a trek up Mount Everest, we would have a route, a guide, gear packed, and supplies. We would research, train, and become conditioned. Our plan would be extremely detailed, but with flexibility built in for unexpected weather conditions, physical illness, equipment failures, bureaucratic red tape, or others getting in our way. We would need to tackle the climb in pieces and ascend slowly: traveling up and then down, from a series of camps. We would expect it to require a sacrifice of time and money.

We may not know every detail of our journeys beyond pain or foresee the obstacles that we'll encounter, but that does not mean that we can't take control of where we are—and where we want to end up. As you slowly traverse the mountains of personal difficulties, this book can be a source of comfort, to help and support you to find new strength and a sense of personal peace. Think of it as your printed guide. Use the following for encouragement:

- It doesn't matter which route I take, as long as I know my destination.

- There is no right or wrong way; it is just ONE of the ways.

- My journey may take longer than someone else's, but it's MY journey.

- My journey will be different from everyone else's because I will have a different view along the way.

- There will be times when my route will be "recalculated." I'll still get there, just in a different way.

Trust that sometimes the worst things that happen to us in life put us directly on the path to the best things that will ever happen to us.

THE SUMMIT—YOUR DESTINATION

Climbing a colossal mountain isn't something people choose to do for the adrenaline rush or on a whim. They are called to the challenge. Something internal has compelled them to climb. Most feel like they have no choice. Given the opportunity, I don't think you would choose to be starting this journey if you could make another choice. It's something that you *have* to do. But where are you headed? What is your ultimate goal?

What does your summit look like? Where do you want to end up? If you can develop a clear vision of what you ultimately want to achieve, it will be easier to identify the steps to get there. Your course will be as unique and complicated as the chaos you find yourself in—but it's the lifeline to get you out. So, what does your destination look like? Here are some examples.

> "THOSE WHO AREN'T CLIMBING TOWARD SOMETHING ARE DESCENDING TOWARD NOTHING."
> RICHARD PAUL EVANS

STORM: DIVORCE
SUMMIT: LOVE MYSELF, MAYBE LOVE AGAIN

A few years ago, I was going through a painful divorce. My goal was to stop hurting. I was in a wretched place and even breathing felt difficult. To somehow stop what had become physical pain was the first summit that came to mind. But my mountain peak was as wide as my pain was deep. Also on my summit: To believe that I was worthy. To get out of bed. To stop crying. To protect my children and help them through the pain *they* were going through. Oh yes! That was a major goal.

And dare I include actually being happy someday? Oh God. And a career—not just a job. I've got to support myself and my kids. So, as long as we are dreaming, I would love to be a content woman working in a field I enjoy. My children would see a mother who was strong, funny, confident, and smart. Bonus, but not integral: a loving partner at the summit with me. Ok. There we go. I have a summit! I was a slobbering, blubbering idiot. But, in the deep recesses of my mind—*that's* what I wanted for myself. And…I had a lot to work with to plan how to reach my summit. Those step-by-step plans became my map. The will to *be* there is important, but the will to *plan* to get there is vital. And, honestly, planning is some of the worst work of the process. It's difficult with no immediate payoff, but it has to be done.

STORM: LAID OFF
SUMMIT: FINANCIAL SECURITY

If you just lost your job—your goal is not necessarily to get a higher paying job with more power and money. That may happen, but setting a destination that is realistic and attainable, will bring you healthy comfort. Break down the various aspects of your summit. That might include: living on a budget, attending school or a training program, living in a home that doesn't financially stress you out. Each aspect of your summit can ultimately lead you to financial security.

STORM: DEATH OF SPOUSE
SUMMIT: RAISE CHILDREN

Maybe you've recently lost your husband and you have two children. Your summit may be to get them through school. Your summit may be to get through until summer, to long days of sunshine, flowers and butterflies. Your journey includes supporting them through their grief. Showing them, by example, how to remember their father with love and honor him by leading a happy and healthy life. That's your summit. For now, you just need to get up every day and drive them to school. Some days, that's all you'll be able to manage. But every day ask yourself: How did I do today? Did I just endure the hours until I climbed back into bed? Did I cry just a little less than yesterday? Did I heal just a fraction of my broken heart? You'll have both good and bad days, and each in its own way will give you the strength tomorrow to take one tiny step forward. Even a tiny step counts to bringing you closer to your summit.

YOUR MAP

Reif Larson wrote, "A map does not just chart, it unlocks and formulates meaning; it forms bridges between here and there, between disparate ideas that we did not know were previously connected." Your map is your route to your summit. And your summit is the disparate ideas woven together and written as your dream destination. Visualize that dream destination. Stephen Covey made this famous when he said, "All things are created twice." First the mental, then the actual. First create the picture, visualize your summit. Then create the steps you'll need to reach it in reality. Those goals are the signposts on your map that lead you to the top. They will keep you from getting lost when the stress of a difficult situation or obstacle can make you forget your plan.

GOAL SETTING

- Details, details, details! What do you really want? Be specific. The more detailed, the easier it is to plan your moves.

- Measurable: make your goals quantitative and measurable. The vaguer they are, the less attainable.

Measurable goals help to track progress in a tangible way.

- Attainable: challenge yourself, but not so much that you become overwhelmed. Challenge brings growth, growth brings change.

- Relevant: what are you willing to work for, what has worked for you in the past? Set your sights on what you believe you can do. Be realistic.

- Time-Bound: save the date. Plan your attack and set a deadline. Don't give yourself too much time; you'll get bored and lose your focus.

Visualize reaching your summit and you can reach it. Set Goal. Make Plan. Get to Work. Stick to it. Reach goal. It's ok to have a meltdown. You are human. Just don't settle in and stay there. Cry it out and then refocus on where you are headed. Break down your ultimate goal into smaller goals. Break down your yearly goals into monthly. Break down your monthly goals into weekly. Assess your weekly goals and break them down into daily goals. What are you going to do today!? By breaking down your ultimate goal into smaller ones—monthly, weekly or daily, you can *see* your success. When you get discouraged, close your eyes and picture yourself after you've overcome the obstacle. Visualizing your success is the key to reaching your goal.

Track your progress. As you work toward your goal, keep a journal, or chart your progress and your setbacks. Set yourself milestones along the way, and make sure to reward yourself for each one. Hold yourself accountable by sharing your goals and milestones. Remind yourself why each goal is important.

What you fight for and struggle with before earning, has the greatest worth. When something is difficult to come by, you'll do that much more to make sure it's even harder to lose. Your goal is worth the struggle, and each moment moves you imperceptibly closer to the journey's end. It will be worth it when you shatter the last obstacle at your feet.

No Turning Back

Commit to your summit. Commitment transforms your goal into reality. A map can lead you to your summit, but you must do the climbing if you wish to get there. Starting is easy. Summiting... not so much. By committing, you give yourself every opportunity to persevere and become creative in the ways you view your journey, overcome obstacles, develop strength, and make progress. Success is a decision. How serious are you about making it to your summit? Are you willing to make it the priority? Achieving even the simplest of goals requires us to learn the meaning of commitment. Without it, you can't achieve anything.

Motivation is what gets you started. Commitment is what keeps you going. To commit, you must fully dedicate yourself to reaching your summit.

> "THERE IS NO ABIDING SUCCESS WITHOUT COMMITMENT."
> TONY ROBBINS

You've already had success in this area! Everything you have ever achieved sprouted from a commitment you made, whether it's your children, job, degree, or buying a house. Learning how to commit is not making commitments, but about keeping those commitments in the face of unforeseen hurdles. What does it mean to you to commit to the summit? Never give up! Never give in.

Career #2
Joe had been laid off from his job at the bank. He wasn't surprised. His heart wasn't in it anymore, and he was burned out. If he was going to work this hard, for these many hours, he wanted to be doing something more meaningful than making more money for a lot of stockholders. What he really wanted to do was work with

seniors. He'd always enjoyed time spent with his grandparents and their friends. He loved hearing their stories, and he hated to see the struggles they had with insurance and care needs. But he had no experience and no idea what kind of job he was qualified to do. With his severance pay and savings, he had about a year to find another job. He took a part-time, entry-level job at a retirement community. His goal was to learn the workings of a senior living community.

Friends and past colleagues scoffed at his choice. "Joe's really hit rock bottom. I heard he's working part-time at a nursing home." Money was tight, and Joe still had bills to pay. But Joe was committed to finding his dream job. A job he could feel good about, helping others, and that he was excited to go to every day. A job with meaning and purpose. At his new job, he got to spend a lot of time with the elders he enjoyed and came to understand their needs. He learned about the variety of jobs he was qualified for in the field that he came to love. His commitment paid off. By the time his year was over, he had designed a new path for himself and several opportunities to pursue in a career where he could feel fulfilled.

There's a difference between being interested and being committed. When you are only interested in doing something, you do it when it is convenient. If the going gets tough, it's easy to give up. When you are committed, you accept no excuses, only results. To commit is to no longer consider possibilities that are inconsistent with the object of your commitment. If your brain is wasting energy traveling down pathways that are not toward your summit, you are not setting yourself up for the highest chance of success. A commitment is simply a really big decision. When you decide something, you are eliminating any other possibilities to consider. You are saying, "I will no longer consider other alternatives. I will only think about ways to accomplish *this* goal." You dedicate all of your energy to succeeding.

The Fable of the Chicken and the Pig (author unknown)
A pig and a chicken are walking down a road. The chicken looks
at the pig and says, "Hey, why don't we open a restaurant?" The
pig looks back at the chicken and says, "Good idea, what do you
want to call it?" The chicken thinks about it and says, "Why don't
we call it 'Ham and Eggs'?" "I don't think so," says the pig. "I'd
be committed, but you'd only be involved."

People who are committed to reaching their summit think:

- I have to get there. What do I need to do to make that happen?

- How have other people gotten to their summit? How have they gotten through this?

- What do I need to change about myself or my life to make this happen?

- What sacrifices do I need to make to get to the summit?

People who are involved or interested but not committed to reaching the summit think:

- I'll try and see how it goes.

- I shouldn't have to do this; go through this. I am the victim.

> "MOST PEOPLE WHO FAIL IN THEIR DREAM, FAIL NOT FROM LACK OF ABILITY BUT FROM LACK OF COMMITMENT."
> ZIG ZIGLAR

- I'll never be happy; I don't really need to summit; It's just too hard.

- I shouldn't have to give up anything. Life's not fair.

Which one are you? Are you ready to map your own journey or give that power away?

Getting It Together

Head Gear
Hand Gear
Sandals
Boots
Socks
Liners
Sleeping Pad
Sleeping Bag
Snow gear
Rain gear
Camping Gear
Don't pack too much
Don't forget anything
Get what you need
Pee Bottle
Pee Bottle?
Sunglasses
Head lamp
Batteries
Chocolate
Backpack
Take everything you need

Don't take too much
Make every piece count
No journey begins without baggage…

THE GEAR

A typical Everest expedition takes 7 - 9 weeks. Climbers need *a lot* of specific gear. An expedition survives on its supplies. The following list is by no means comprehensive but can give you an idea of the amount of equipment required.

Footwear: Climbing boots; cold weather boots for base camp; running shoes and/or trail shoes; sport sandals; lightweight hiking boots; gaiters; booties; lightweight socks; midweight/heavy socks; liner socks

Clothing: Lightweight long underwear top; expedition-weight long underwear tops; lightweight long underwear bottoms; expedition-weight underwear bottoms; briefs; short-sleeved shirts; synthetic or fleece jacket; synthetic insulated pants; down suit; down insulated jacket with hood; down pants; waterproof, breathable jacket and pants; wind shirts/ light shell jacket; one piece climbing shell

Head & Hand Gear: Liner gloves; wind stopper fleece gloves; insulated climbing gloves; mittens with liners; bandana; sun hat; wool or fleece hat; heavy and light balaclava; face mask

Accessories: sunglasses; glacier glasses; ski goggles; headlamp with spare bulb; spare batteries

Climbing Equipment: Ice axe; crampons; harness; carabiners; webbing; Perion cord; Ascenders; rappel device

Camping Gear: Backpack; daypack; two sleeping bags; compression stuff sacks; sleeping pad; foam pad; water bottles; lightweight steel thermal bottle; pee bottle; pack towel; trekking poles; swiss army knife; large mug, plastic bowl, fork and spoon

Medical & Personal: Sunscreen; lip screen; toiletry kit; first-aid kit; water purification tablets; Ziploc bags; antiseptic wipes; ear plugs

Travel items: expedition duffel bag; small travel bag; nylon stuff sacks; lightweight long sleeve shirt; hiking pants; lightweight pants

BAGGAGE

As with the undertaking of any important expedition, we must be properly prepared, so we need to spend a few moments taking inventory of our gear. Each of us carries with us our own mis-matched set of baggage. Our experiences, our trials, our tribulations. Our scars, our past, and our sorrows. We have protective behaviors, defense mechanisms, and beliefs about ourselves that we've learned in the past. Some of our baggage is useful and healthy, some we carry around with us because, well, we always have. It's familiar. It's who we are. It's comfortable.

That may be true, but sometimes we need to take a closer look at what we are carrying. On a mountain trek, every piece of gear in our backpack needs to earn its place. Extra baggage weighing us down will impede success. So, it's time to examine our baggage and see if we need to do a little repacking. What we are looking for are tools we need on our journey. If possible, lighten the load and throw a few things out. But we may also need to do a little shopping.

> "THESE MOUNTAINS THAT YOU ARE CARRYING, YOU WERE ONLY SUPPOSED TO CLIMB."
> NAJWA ZEBIAN

I HATE the Carry-on
When was the last time you flew somewhere? Did you check your bags—for a price these days, or use a carry-on? Let me repeat: I HATE the carry-on! Yes, I have one. One with a collapsible

handle, rotating rollers, clips to attach OTHER bags to it. I drag it behind me through security. Load it, reload it. Stand by while it's examined by TSA wearing gloves and poking wands through it. I drag it through the Starbucks line. Take it to the bathroom with me. And essentially, stress out about it until I am seated on the plane and have found room in the overhead for it. I want to go back to the days when I could just check my damn bag. I could bring as many pairs of shoes as I wanted and not worry if my luggage was too heavy to carry. I could roam the airport for a few short hours of care-free, happy-go-lucky, 'I don't have any baggage' bliss! Surely, I'm not the only one who feels this way? Just drop it all off somewhere where someone else can be in charge of it? It would be nice. But even the airlines find unclaimed baggage. They track you down, sometimes in the middle of the night, and leave it on your doorstep.

Since we can't escape it, let's take a closer look at what kind of baggage we are carrying. If it's not earning its place, we need to let it go.

THESE BAGS FLY FREE—INTERNAL 'GEAR'

1. A Positive Attitude

We cannot control the inevitability of events that put us on this journey, but we can influence their effects in our life by adjusting our attitude toward them. Being positive on the trek is one of the most valuable approaches to help us keep taking steps forward, when all we want to do is turn around. It's not physical toughness, but mental toughness that will inspire us. A positive thought is 100 times more powerful than a negative thought. Don't let your mind get stuck in the negative.

> "YOUR ATTITUDE, NOT YOUR APTITUDE, WILL DETERMINE YOUR ALTITUDE."
> ZIG ZIGLAR

The Power of Positivity
A 90-year-old moved into our assisted living community. She was elegant, well-dressed, and charming. She was also almost completely blind. Her husband of 60-plus years had just died, and she wasn't safe to live alone. As she walked into the community, I described her surroundings. "I love it," she said excitedly. "Wait until we see your room." I told her. "It doesn't matter," she said. "Happiness is something you decide on ahead of time. Whether I like my room or not doesn't depend on the furniture or the food. It's all in how I choose to feel about it. I already decided to love it. It's a decision I make every morning. I figure I can spend the day moping about my life or I can get up and be thankful for what I still have. Each day is a gift. As long as I remember that, I'll be happy."

2. Belief

We've talked about this. Belief sustains the journey. If you believe, you will get there. You must cultivate a fierce belief in yourself. Your true self—the self that is whole, the self that is enough and the self that no longer looks to others for definition, completion, or approval. When that belief develops into conviction, when it is anchored in your soul and nothing can destroy it, then belief becomes faith. And faith in yourself is a powerful force. The power of faith in ourselves allows us to push beyond the seemingly impossible. It pulls us through when all evidence suggests that we quit.

Unstoppable
Maya's ex didn't think she could do it. Survive without him. He saw her as weak, dependent, inexperienced. Frustrated and disgusted, Maya thought, "Doesn't he know me at all?" Obviously not. In this case, Maya's belief in herself was fueled by anger. And, that's ok. Sometimes we need that kind of fuel to propel us to go the distance. Maya was so hurt and angry that her husband had so little faith in her, who she was and what she was capable

of—that she wanted to prove how wrong he was. She believed she was unstoppable, and so she was.

3. Will

There's no room for excuses. The adage, "Where there's a will, there's a way," whether it's over, under, around or through—is true. If you ferociously want to heal, grow, and thrive, you have to keep going. You must cultivate a strong will and conviction. It may take reading an inspiring saying that you post on your bathroom mirror and recite in the morning or at bedtime. A reminder such as: I love myself and I am worth fighting for; I will allow myself to move into a healthy, satisfying, joyful phase of life. Trust that with each trial, you will emerge stronger, surer, and more deserving of the dream itself. Your desire to summit will take you there.

I Will be Number One
Steve Roland "Pre" Prefontaine was an American middle and long-distance runner who competed in the 1972 Olympics. Prefontaine once held the American record in seven different distance track events, from the 2,000 meters to the 10,000 meters. He died in 1975. He is still considered one of the greatest American runners in history. He was popular for his accomplishments, but also for his all-out running style and outspoken opinions. Pre didn't believe in pacing himself during a race, he gave it his all from start to finish. One of his many famous quotes about running demonstrates his strong will. "A lot of people run a race to see who is fastest. I run to see who has the most guts, who can punish himself into an exhausting pace, and then at the end, punish himself even more."

4. Perseverance

The power of tenacity. Persevere, no matter what the challenges. Refuse to quit and one cannot fail. Every obstacle we encounter is a natural and necessary step on the journey to reaching our summit. In the Greek language, the word perseverance is literally made up of two words. One means "to remain." The other word means "under." That tells us that perseverance is the ability to be steadfast under the pressure of difficulty. Add in a dose of resilience—and there is your winning combo! Not only do you have the strength to persist, but the ability to start over. Practice overcoming hurdles in everyday life. As you nurture your ability to recover quickly from difficulties, your mental power of perseverance is strengthened. When the going gets tough, the tough remain. Have you ever listened to the words of that Simon and Garfunkel song about the boxer? "I am leaving. I am leaving, but the fighter still remains." Be the fighter. Maybe you will have to change course, but don't give up. Effort only fully releases its reward after a person refuses to quit.

57 Marathons in 52 weeks
My husband ran 57 Marathons in 52 weeks. Yes, that means there were some weekends that he ran two marathons in one weekend. All while working a full-time job and driving around the country to marathons every weekend. Sometimes he would arrive back into town just in time to drive straight to work on a Monday morning. He was inspired by running programs in inner cities for disadvantaged teens. He hoped that by doing something big, he could bring awareness to those types of programs and more would be developed. That was his WHY. But, more incredibly, HOW? How did he do it? How could he keep his body moving for hours on end, over, and over, and over again? He simply wouldn't quit. Through illness, injury, and disappointment, he persevered. He refused all alternatives. He. Would. Not. Quit.

5. Humor
   Humor is so important we are going to talk about it at length in another chapter. But it bears mentioning here, as

part of our day-to-day gear, or even our armor. In fact, I never leave home without it.

Never underestimate the power of laughter; and if you aren't there yet, and the best you can possibly manage is a smile, that's good too. There is scientific proof that using the facial muscles required to make the corners of our mouths turn up—actually contributes to chemical reactions in our bodies to release endorphins—which make us feel happier. "Fake it until you make it." Sometimes that's all we can do—but on the inside, our bodies are working to help us along.

Do you know who's really funny? Me!
A few years ago, I reconnected with some old friends. As I got together with the old gang, someone said, "You are still so funny!" Huh? Is that how people saw me? I was funny? Did I even remember that I was funny? Is that how people used to think of me? I don't think anyone who had known me in the past few years would describe me as funny. When did I lose that? Was it repeatedly frowned upon until it no longer existed as a part of my identity? Never again! I will never let others take away who I am, or one of the things I value most about myself. I am funny, and I love to laugh.

SUIT UP! EXTERNAL GEAR

Some days I don't get dressed
Most days I want to stay in bed or on the couch
Grab that ratty green sweater for comfort and protection
But survival doesn't exist within the perimeter of the bed
I'm going to have to venture forth
Out of bed
Out of the house
Out of my comfort zone
On my path
I'll need armor to protect myself

1. Armor

Do you have a favorite robe or well-worn sweater that you put on when you're sick because it gives you comfort? Of course, you do. We all do. We have lucky socks, power suits, a favorite dress. Your 'sassy' date jacket. Your 'interview' tie. Your power t-shirt for demanding, strenuous workouts at the gym. These items are the armor we clothe ourselves in when we need strength for heading into a challenge. Well—open up the closet and dig deep. You need all of the armor you own right now!

"Hello, Old Friend"

You think I've run into someone from my past? Not so! You've heard of comfort food? Let's talk about comfort clothes. I'm talking about that fuzzy pink bathrobe your kids always make fun of or your favorite college sweatshirt that you still wear, even though the cuffs are frayed and stains adorn the front of it. Here is one time when I was desperate for mine: My mother was gone. I didn't get there in time. I came home and threw the closet door open in a frenzy to find the green sweater I had worn for weeks. The one my kids had insisted I banish to the back of my closet. My need was almost obsessive. I HAD to have it. It had become my security blanket. With its matted sleeves, ripped hem, and balls of shredded wool—that itchy mess enveloped me in familiarity and security no hug could ever replace. I was going to be ok. And, as I stood there in that sweater, a sense of calm came over me. I needed this simple creature comfort to balance the emotional turmoil of losing my mom.

2. Knowledge

Knowledge is the most powerful tool you can own. Find it, use it, hoard it.

If you have cancer, find out about it. What kind is it, what can trigger it, what do 'other' doctors say about it? Treatments, medications, alternative treatments, diet. I am astounded every time I hear someone say, "The doctor said I need to see a specialist. I don't know why. I forget what kind. They are going to run some tests. Not sure which ones." You're not the doctor, nor do you play one on TV. But, you're not stupid. Learn everything you can. Remember: when we feel stressed, it's important to make lists to keep track of our thoughts. Write down questions for the professionals, no matter how insignificant they seem.

What don't you know about? How to assemble a trampoline? Applying for a mortgage? Taxes? What insurance you need? Money management? Investments? Fixing the sink? Drug interactions? Writing a resume? Alternative medications? Re-training programs? You don't know what you don't know. Read books, attend a workshop. With today's resources and technology, you can learn anything. Even directions to the computer store to figure out how to get online.

Google to the Rescue!
Eva's husband had always taken care of the house repairs and even finished their basement for the kids. When he suddenly died at 47, she had her hands full with three kids, a job, and house on her own. With his insurance, she was able to keep the house, but there was little room in the budget for maintenance or repairs. When the upstairs sink was leaking through to the kitchen ceiling, she panicked. The first plumber she called charged $150 just to come take a look. She didn't have it! But she did have her husband's tools. She would have to figure it out. Google to the rescue! After some research and watching several YouTube videos, Eva could see that the problem wasn't that drastic. She turned off the water, found the right wrench, and followed the video.

3. Expertise, Please!
Bring in the experts. Counselors, financial advisors, career advisors, medical and mental health professionals, mentors,

ministers, priests, rabbis, support groups. They're out there, people. Find them!

PTSD
Grant is in the Army. His unit has been deployed twice in the past three years—once to Iraq and once to Afghanistan. Grant has seen his share of firefights. Several times he came close to death from nearby explosions. Some of his friends weren't so lucky. Grant tried to leave those memories overseas when he came home, but it didn't work. He would wake up at night in a panic, reliving the attacks. He tried self-medicating with alcohol. He broke up with his girlfriend. He avoided his family. Grant is most likely suffering from Post-Traumatic Stress Disorder. He can't fix this on his own. He needs help from a specialist in this field.

BAG CHECK!

What gear do you possess, and what shopping needs to be done? You may have enough to get started. Perhaps you'll need to pick up a few things along the way. However, everything in your bag must earn its place or you need to leave it behind.

WHO'S IN YOUR CAMP?

Why am I here?
This load is too heavy
This place is too frightening
It's not real. Not normal. I am in a graveyard of ice
I'm in unknown territory
I've never been this terrified
I feel my heart slamming into my throat
I have metal spikes strapped to my boots. I can't walk
I cannot breathe
It's too much
Stop
It's too much
Please don't make me do this
The crevasse is thirty feet wide, so deep that no bottom is visible.
A great, yawning chasm of darkness. I am balanced precariously
on an aluminum ladder – one of four lashed together to span the
gap. My crampons scrape against the first aluminum rung, and
I am frozen. The icy flush of terror paralyzes my limbs, leaving
me with a dizzying sense of free fall. But if I fall, there will be
no help. Trapped in an alien realm of ice, I will be lost forever
"Don't look down."
But down is the only place to look

"Come, friend. Come with me."
Sherpas carrying enormous loads want to squeeze past me
"Follow."
They are barely breathing hard despite the enormous packs they
carry. These are the people employed to ferry the gear and supplies
to the high camps in the mountains. These are the people who
lashed the ladders together, strung the rope lines. They are the
guides through the vast unknown
I have to follow
One step
Breathe
Step
Breathe
I will follow

SHERPAS

Atop Everest, your own preparation and training will support you to successfully make it to your summit. But as we all can attest (hence, my writing and your reading this book), the unexpected happens. Your only rescue squad are the others who take on the mountain with you. Your Sherpas. Technically, Sherpas are an ethnic group of people in Tibet. The first Everest climbers, in the early twentieth century, realized the importance of Sherpas to mountaineering expeditions. Since Sherpas have lived at high altitudes for generations, they are genetically stronger when closer to the clouds than are their sea-level counterparts. They've become specialists in assisting alpine expeditions in the Himalayan Mountains. Climbers are not only impressed with their abilities, but also their spirits.

Some people glorify the Sherpas as natural gods of nature, with stronger abilities than those possessed by the average human. They are mystical, pure of heart, powerful, accomplished guides with endurance, experience, and resilience. An excellent example of the benefit of different specialists for different situations. These are the people we want to be surrounded by on our journeys. Our mountain may not be Everest, but Sherpas are the gift we can give ourselves to reach our summits.

WHY BUILD A TEAM?

Even in climbing, there can be a stigma about asking for or using help. Hiring Sherpas. Or not using bottled oxygen. But we are not professionals. We are not setting a world record in pain and suffering. Sometimes it takes a crisis to teach us that we don't have to do it alone; shouldn't have to do it alone. Jeff Bauman, who lost both legs in the Boston Marathon bombing in 2013 urged survivors of catastrophic events to accept help being offered by friends and loved ones. "Trust the people around you. Use your support group," Bauman told Megyn Kelly on *The Today Show* in October 2017. "That's huge, because usually when people go through something traumatic, you tend to isolate a lot, and I did in my recovery." He went on to say, "I isolated a lot and pushed people away from me that were trying to help. So, I would just recommend that you don't isolate and that you work on both your physical and mental recovery."

There is no shame in assistance. Teams strengthen the cause, and right now—the cause is you and your journey. You *need* to build a support team of friends, colleagues, family, advisors, and mentors. A highly trained special unit of allies and accomplices with a variety of skills and diverse talents. Sometimes small. Sometimes large. But always strong enough to support you emotionally, and knowledgeable enough to guide you to success. Your personal support team will benefit you with a wide range of abilities—psychologically and sometimes physically, and keep you accountable when you stumble or lose your way.

Inventory existing contacts and identify role models for strength and inspiration. Find others to "believe" with you and ask for help! Though you may lean on your friends, some will be Sherpas and others will not. It doesn't make them any less important or change your friendship. But, with Sherpas, you are relying on the diverse talents and skill sets that they provide you through your journey. An acquaintance or friend of a friend may become a Sherpa. Some you may not even know yet. As you are thinking about who your Sherpas may be, keep in mind that you'll need both: knowledgeable support (your experts), and emotional support. No one achieves greatness by themselves.

EMOTIONAL SUPPORT

The quality and quantity of understanding support you receive on your journey will have a major impact on your success. You cannot, and you should not, try to do this alone. Having someone rooting for your well-being and reminding you of the good in your life is an effective way to stay on track. Talking to someone who is truly supportive can build self-confidence. It can be a friend you trade positive text messages with every day, or the group that meets once a month. Surrounding yourself with supportive, positive people can increase your odds of staying positive and reaching your goal. To be truly helpful, the people in your support system must appreciate the impact of what you are going through. Look for those rare people who ask you how you are…and wait to hear the answer.

FOR OUR HEALTH

Social support not only assists us on our journeys, but it's an important part of a person's well-being. A study at the Mayo Clinic finds that friendships improve our health by:

- Increasing a sense of belonging and purpose
- Boosting happiness

- Reducing stress
- Improving feelings of self-worth
- Helping us to cope with trauma
- Encouraging us to change or avoid unhealthy lifestyle habits

Research proves that social interaction affects the immune system as well. Lack of it can negatively lead to the first signs of depression and anxiety. However, they are not sure about which comes first: depression or social isolation. With life-threatening conditions such as cancer or HIV/AIDS, a strong social network can aid in recovery and improve one's quality of life—extremely important for the mental health of a seriously ill person. The vital takeaway: People need People!

BUT NOT NEGATIVE PEOPLE!

Think of life like an elevator: on your way up, you may have to stop and let certain people off. Sometimes it's easier to find support from a complete stranger or a new friend. They don't carry preconceived ideas about what you can or cannot do. What you should or shouldn't do. They simply support what you are trying to achieve. You are the company you keep. Consciously focus on the positive feeling of support until belief in yourself registers in your subconscious and manifests in how you think and feel every day. Your Sherpas will support your focus.

KNOWLEDGEABLE SUPPORT

Mentors provide invaluable insight into changes on the route that will get you to the summit. A guide who has traveled the same path can accompany you at intervals along the way, initiating small corrections in direction. You might be blind to inherent dangers that exist or shortcuts to consider. In the end, guides can save you a lot of wasted steps. This support may come from friends, acquaintances or professionals you hire to get you what you need.

MY SHERPAS

I honor my personal Sherpas with my eternal gratitude. I have a Sherpa for Experience, Power, Spirituality, Blue Skies, Mojo, Loyalty, Laughter, and Inspiration. Sherpas change with the ebb and flow of life. Let me introduce you to a few of the Sherpas who have helped me on my journey.

Experienced Sherpa Diana set the pace after college graduation by finding a job first. She was the first to get married, the first to own a home, the first to become a mother, and the first to get divorced. The die was cast. Diana is my "Experienced" Sherpa. The Expert. The Advisor. The Survivor. Diana knew how to land a man, run a home, and be a mom. She went from Lady Di, Princess of our posse; to Dr. Di: authority on all things important—and I went to her with every question.

Di, can I have the recipe for those cream cheese brownies?

Di, what should I serve at a bridal shower?

Bills? How do I keep track of all of these?

Pregnancy? Childbirth?

Diana, how do I treat RSV, chicken pox, vaccines, fevers?

I can't stop crying. If I get meds for this, can he use it against me to get the kids?

Lawyers? Maintenance? Child support? Taxes?

For every curve in the road, Diana has always been there before me. I couldn't have gotten through life without her sound advice, resources, and hours and hours of telephone counseling. Forever the practical one, Di is always available to advise me WHAT to do. Coincidence? I don't think so.

Loyal Sherpa While Diana settled into her "adult" life, Paige and I were Divas of the 80s—flaunting our giant earrings, big hair and shoulder pads.

We finally grew up and into relationships that changed our lives. Continuing to live fairly near to each other, we were loyal friends—through weddings, careers, and babies. Her lake house became our retreat and offered respite from the adult life... And like the "loyal" wife she was and is, Paige followed her husband to the coast, so he could pursue his dreams. It seems like yesterday that we were enjoying our final weekend at the lake. I tearfully drove home, thinking about her new life on the West Coast and crying over losing my best friend. I walked into my house, lost and sad, only to find out that a best friend moving across the country was not the worst thing that could happen.

The storm had broken, and it was the most horrific time of my life. Life's brought other storms, but this felt catastrophic. Maybe because I didn't have the skills I needed when the first one hit, but thank goodness, I had Sherpas. From across the country, Paige helped hold the shattered pieces of my world together. I was not surviving. I was barely existing. Paige kept me breathing. She is the truest of friends. Listening to me, crying with me, and pointing out a few harsh realities. How or why she kept answering the phone, I'll never know. But Paige was the lifeline I needed during the worst storm of my life.

Spiritual Sherpa Marie and I met when her son and mine became friends in first grade. I felt intimidated by Marie and her family. She was, and had, everything I thought I was lacking. She has several sisters; her mom was her best friend. They were the closest family I had ever seen. Beautiful. Intelligent. Trendy. Always smiling. Close. Close. Close. One was never alone. And their love for each other was palpable.

Marie, the oldest, was surely the leader of these ladies, but not by force. Marie exudes quiet grace. She possesses a natural beauty that shines from within. Always showing love. Never passing judgement. Never drawing undue attention to herself. Full of the most obvious common sense that fulfills her priorities, which never waiver. From a Christian perspective, when you hear that Christ manifests himself in the people around you, I see that in Marie. God shows me Jesus in her every smile.

So, there we were: the princess and the court jester—on a path that neither of us expected. I remember our first serious conversation, beyond, "Hi, your son is such a sweet boy." We were working the same volunteer shift at a school function, and I was fretting and stressed about something. Anything. It didn't really matter. I was constantly getting worked up.

After listening to me carry on, Marie said, "Oh, I never worry about stuff like that. Things always seem to work out." What?! Was she nuts? Didn't worry?! It was Wednesday… How could she not know what they were doing for the weekend and which birthday party they would go to on Saturday afternoon? Was she insane? Didn't she *care*?? What did she mean, everything always works out? Not in *my* world it didn't!

And that became one of the defining conversations of my life. One of the great secrets had been revealed. I was not in control. I recognize my spiritual Sherpa as being instrumental on my journey by teaching me that my life is divinely guided, and I believe she was used by Christ to help me learn this lesson. Regardless of your personal religious or spiritual tradition, gratitude for those who enlighten us about existence is universal.

Power Sherpa Laura is the Sherpa that I hadn't even met when my storm broke. Ironically, that hasn't stopped her from becoming my 'vault,' the one to whom I confide *all* the intimate secrets of my sordid world. True to form, each of my Sherpas had a *piece* of my story. I've typically held back. I've usually kept a few secrets. But, as with all of my Sherpas,

God puts people in my life for a reason. Through Laura, I learned to trust. To let myself be vulnerable. And in giving myself over completely to her—including flaws and failures, I've been given back the power to handle it all.

Laura and I met through a direct marketing pyramid. Yes, I actually did that, and more than once. When we started working together, I was a lost soul, trying to make a dime and keep my family together. Laura and I got into the habit of meeting for coffee to discuss business. We spent hours talking and laughing about anything BUT business. Nothing was sacred. Our conversations bounced between defective products, to troubled kids, to TV. Trips we wanted to earn, food we had to eat, and crazy coworkers we had to endure. Building a sales empire, selling a house—I've never laughed so hard in my life! But what we came back to over and over, besides the humor, was the power. The power of believing in myself.

Through business, we were exposed to leadership training about feeling empowered or inspiring others to be. Combine that with our own research to find enlightenment, and we were linked. Laura has the gift of empowerment. She knows her strengths and isn't afraid to embrace them. She can welcome imperfect moments and know that she has the knowledge, confidence and ability to be in control of her own life and take on her biggest dreams. And when her batteries run low, I've been there for the jumpstart she needs as a reminder.

I can't remember the first time she looked me in the eye and said, "You are a powerful woman." But I remember distinctly the day we were having coffee and she said, "You're not happy." I was fighting a divorce, begging for a reconciliation. It was misery, and it was time to give in. Thank goodness for my Sherpas.

Less and less became taboo to share as I poured my inner thoughts and feelings into Laura's listening ears. When one of us dared to tread into dangerous waters, it was with love and trust and laughter. One time, I called crying. She listened with sympathy for a few minutes before saying, "How much longer are you going to feel sorry for yourself?" What? Did she need coffee? But that sincerity was exactly what I needed. She snapped me out of it. After snuffling a bit, I answered that I was almost done, and could I have just a couple more minutes...

Today, I can't remember what I was so upset about, but I remember how my Sherpa Laura helped me find power from within. We moved apart after that, but she left me a legacy of empowerment; and besides, I learned long ago that friends don't have to be close, to be close.

The best kinds of people come into your life and make you see sunshine where you once saw clouds. People who believe in you so totally, you start to believe in you, too. People who love you for simply being you. Once in a lifetime kind of people. I hope the descriptions of a few of my Sherpas help you to identify your own and realize the power and support that you gain from them.

TIPS FOR SHERPAS

Because deep relationships are reciprocal; we may be someone else's Sherpa.

- Be there.

- Be willing to listen.

- Acknowledge their loss.

- Don't judge.

- Answer questions honestly. You don't need to have all of the answers.

- It's ok to say, "I don't know what to say."

- Encourage normal activities and routine.
- Offer to spend time with your friend.
- Offer a hug.
- Allow time—don't expect the journey to end quickly.
- Ask them how they are doing at different times.
- Take care of yourself.

Sherpas are your guides on this journey. They may be existing friends, acquaintances, or people you meet along the way. Only you know who your Sherpas are and who you need to get you to the summit.

THE TREK

Screeeeech?
Screeeeech!
20,000 feet
Aluminum ladders strapped together
Frozen spikes strapped to my boots
Screeeeech
One misstep, one small error
Mooooaaannn
Seracs the size of office buildings are shifting and moaning
They can crush you in an instant
No warning
An eerie blue labyrinth
Blue because the ice is so dense only one color of the spectrum is reflected
I'm climbing
Blood, sweat and icy tears
Every aspect of this climb is an assault on the mountain
I'm on a mountain
Beautiful
Scary
Scraaape. My crampon spikes scrape against an aluminum ladder
Head down. One step at a time
Screeech
Over the ladders, but not out of the Ice Fall
Step. Scratch. Scrape

Moooooaaaan
Screeeeech
20 more steps
Screeech
10
One foot in front of the other
One step at a time
Inch by inch
I can see safety
A sudden, desperate longing washes over me to be there
8, 7, 6 steps. 5, 4, 3, 2
Safety
Look at me!
I am a mountaineer!
I did it!

I only have to do it 5 more times...

THE KHUMBA ICEFALL

The Khumba Icefall is an icefall located at the foot of the Lhotse Face of Mt. Everest. No part of the Everest route is more feared by climbers. The icefall is considered one of the most dangerous stages of the South Col (Nepal) route to Everest's summit. It is estimated that the glacier advances 3 to 4 feet down the mountain every day. The icefall, moving at that speed, opens large crevasses with little warning, and the large towers of ice (seracs), can topple over suddenly. Some say it is the most technically demanding section of the route. For this reason, guides and Sherpas blaze a zigzag path through the ice towers using a mile of rope and something like 60 aluminum ladders.

The moaning is the sound of the glacier shifting, ice shattering, and water rumbling. From Mount Everest Base Camp, climbers must pass through the Khumbu Icefall. They can *only* traverse this area with the aid of ropes and ladders. Even with all of the safety precautions, this section is extremely dangerous. Shifting ice, deep crevasses, falling ice, and avalanches have killed many climbers and Sherpas. Most climbers must navigate the Khumbu Icefall at least twice, and sometimes more, as they acclimate to the elevation.

We are treading on new ground and unfamiliar territory. It may not be level, solid, necessarily smooth, or free of debris. We may stumble and fall. There are bound to be pitfalls on parts of our path. We have one job: keep moving. Do not lose focus, even when it's scary. Forget what lies behind and reach forward to what lies ahead. Press on toward the summit.

Discouragement—Our Personal Icefall

Someone said that one of the world's deadliest diseases was discouragement. That seems odd, but the more I thought about it, the more I could see the point.

- It's universal. We all get discouraged from time to time.

- It's recurring. Discouragement is not necessarily a one-time thing. We may suffer from it over and over again.

- It's highly contagious. Our discouragement can rub off on other people. Theirs can rub off on us!

Why Do People Get Discouraged?

1. The first cause of discouragement is fatigue. We get tired! Why is life so dang hard? Shouldn't it be easier than this? Haven't I been down this road? I'm sick of working through the pain. Dealing with the feelings, building new relationships! The payoff is slow and

the journey is long. Do you know when we are apt to get discouraged the most? When we're halfway through a project. Everyone works hard at first, but when the newness wears off and life settles into a rut, discouragement can take over.

2. The second cause of discouragement is frustration. When we focus on the obstacles instead of the goal, we run the risk of discouragement.

3. The third cause of discouragement is failure. The difference between winners and losers is that winners always see failure as only a temporary setback.

4. The fourth cause of discouragement is fear. When our discouragement is caused by fear—whether fear of embarrassment, criticism, or failure, we feel a deep, intense desire to run. That's because the natural reaction to fear is flee; to want to escape.

So, get the F out of here. The F of fatigue, frustration, failure, and fear. Discouragement is actually curable. When we feel discouraged to the point of wanting to give up, we can do three things to remedy the situation: reorganize, remember, and resist. Our Rx, if you will.

Reorganize - don't give up on your goals. Devise a new approach. We may be doing the right thing but doing it in the wrong way.

Job Search
After her divorce, Jeanine had looked for a job for months, without success. She was desperate to start earning the money she needed to support herself and her children. Working a retail job at the mall was the last option she wanted to consider, but she needed something. She continued to pursue her goal of a job in Human Resources around her retail schedule. Once she was back in the workforce (even though it was at the mall), the routine and

positive feedback boosted her self-esteem. Her interviewing skills improved—she was less nervous, and employers saw her abilities and confidence. She eventually had to choose between two jobs in her field.

Remember - to recommit yourself to your summit. Remember, our thoughts determine our feelings. If we feel discouraged, it could be due to thinking discouraging thoughts. If we'd rather feel encouraged, be mindful of thinking encouraging thoughts. Visual reminders can help keep us focused on where we want to be. Ask yourself: did I make a dream-board, a collage, a picture of myself at my summit? Keep that on hand for tough times, to remind you where you are headed. Paste those inspirational quotes on the mirror; repeat positive affirmations three times a day. Remember how far you've come; not just how far you have left to go. You are not where you want to be, but neither are you where you used to be!

Resist - discouragement is a choice. If we choose to, we can give in to it. Or, we can choose to resist the temptation and refuse to be discouraged. Don't give up, even in the face of fatigue, frustration, fear, or failure. And, if experiencing a bad week or weekend—that's ok. Take a step back to acknowledge how you are feeling, regroup, and start again.

We must proceed like a dedicated mountain climber who spots a previously unknown and seemingly unreachable peak. She is at once attracted to its majesty and excited by the promise of its lofty secrets, but reluctant to begin her ascent because she knows it will be challenging. However, her love of the climb outweighs the fear of falling, and so she brushes away the last thought of difficulty. She understands that all she needs to do to reach new heights is to study the slope and start to climb.

STUDY THE SLOPE

Sustaining motivation can be tough even in the best of circumstances. If achieving goals was quick and easy, everyone would be doing it.

- Visualize your goal—down to the most insightful detail.

- List the reasons you want to accomplish your goal.

- Set milestones and rewards. Neuroscience tells us that each small success triggers the brain's reward center, releasing the feel-good chemical dopamine. This helps focus our concentration and inspires us to take another similar step.

- Be prepared to change your route. There will be obstacles. Unexpected setbacks and storms. Don't be surprised. They *will* happen.

- Get help! Professional or part of your team. This is why you have Sherpas.

- Have a plan for waning motivation. How will you re-energize? Keep yourself going? Give yourself breaks? Don't be too hard on yourself.

CLIMB

Keep moving forward. Don't look too far ahead. Speed doesn't matter. Forward is forward. Persistence is everything on our journey. We must persist, even if it is only with our wish to be persistent. Persistence is the grace that allows us to continue to move forward even when we are stuck in hell. I love Winston Churchill's words, "If you are going through hell, keep on going." This exemplifies the steadfast pursuit of trudging forward until the hell looks less scary and the route seems more defined.

Remember the movie *What about Bob?* Richard Dreyfus is a therapist whose book on Baby Steps has Bob Murray taking "baby steps" all over the therapist's family vacation. Not a bad theory! Baby steps to the grocery store. Baby steps to the job interview. Baby steps to the doctor's appointment. The goal is progress, not perfection or speed. Just enough pace to keep up a certain momentum. Our intention put into action will keep the steps coming.

Someone said persistence is the hard work you do after you get tired of doing the hard work you already did. Persistence is guts. It says: don't give up. We need to keep moving forward in spite of the forces that seem to be against us. Our only need is to want the summit more than the alternative. If it's important enough, we'll find a way. If not, we will find an excuse.

> "ADOPT THE PACE OF NATURE, HER SECRET IS PATIENCE."
> RALPH WALDO EMERSON

Degree

Dana is working on her college degree. I asked her when she would finish, and she laughed. Oh, I don't know. I should have been done a long time ago, but I can only take classes when I have the time, the right class is offered when I'm available, and, of course, when I have the money to pay for it. I'm working a full-time job and two part-time jobs, but I haven't given up. The quiet steadiness of persistence is powerfully propelling her to her goal.

Be patient. Don't think about what can happen in a year or a month. Focus on the 24 hours in front of you, and do what you can to get closer to where you want to be. Just keep moving.

Aesop's Famous Fable of The Hare and the Tortoise
The Hare was once boasting of his speed before the other animals.
"I have never yet been beaten," said he, "when I put forth my full
speed. I challenge anyone here to race with me." The Tortoise said
quietly, "I accept your challenge." "That is a good joke," said the
Hare; "I could dance round you all the way." "Keep your boast-
ing till you've beaten," answered the Tortoise. "Shall we race?" A
course was fixed and a start was set. The Hare darted almost out
of sight at once, but soon stopped; and to show his contempt for
the Tortoise, lay down to have a nap. The Tortoise plodded on and
plodded on, and when the Hare awoke from his nap, he saw the
Tortoise near the winning-post and could not run up in time to
save the race. Then said the Tortoise: "Plodding wins the race."

CELEBRATE SUCCESSES

It pays to acknowledge small wins. Alcoholics Anonymous
doesn't ask its members to never drink again—that goal would
probably seem unreachable. It asks them not to drink *that
day*, and it recognizes small milestones by awarding 'sobriety
coins,' usually monthly, for periods of abstinence. Take a lesson from this practice and find ways to celebrate incremental
achievements. Concentrate on small victories.

Replace a negative thought with a positive thought.
Celebrate!

Walk 30 minutes. Celebrate!

Eat dinner alone. Celebrate!

Meet with a financial planner to review what your spouse
had always handled. Celebrate!

Journal about your day. Celebrate!

Tackle your late wife's closet. Celebrate!

Stick to the consequence you gave your teenager. Celebrate!

Say NO to an event you don't really want to attend.
Celebrate!

Make an appointment with a counselor. Celebrate!

Spend twenty minutes on your resume. Celebrate!

Recognizing accomplishments is vital. We don't have to wait until we've reached our goal to be proud of ourselves. Be proud of *every* step taken toward reaching that goal. Celebrating the small advances we make helps us to stay motivated and to realize our potential.

One of the best reasons to celebrate success is simply that it feels good. When we celebrate with good feelings, more good feelings arise. We want these changes in our lives because we want to feel better, happier. Success lies at the heart of it. A large part of success is about one's state of mind—so it's about having a success mindset. And this success mindset requires cultivation. Yes, techniques like affirmations and visualization have a part to play, but celebrating our success is another tool for cultivating this way of thinking about our progress.

Focus on what's been accomplished, rather than on what's not working or a long, overwhelming list of what's yet to do. Tell yourself: 'I am successful' or 'I can do this because I've succeeded before,' to build up self-belief and a success attitude. Downplaying our success, or not acknowledging our steps forward may be telling ourselves we haven't done enough, or we don't deserve to celebrate. Whereas when we notice and celebrate our advances, we begin to see ourselves as someone who is successful rather than someone who is trying to *become* successful.

LET ME CATCH
MY BREATH

Sleep is elusive on the mountain, and I am tired
I am tired
I keep coughing
What's wrong with me? Flu?
I am so tired...
Can't breathe. Can't get enough air
Step. My brain is in slow motion
Step
I am even too tired to think
Who is that who keeps coughing?
Step
Stumble
Cough. I feel light-headed, like I drank too much
Step
A coughing fit sends shards of glass through my throat and lungs
Another agonizing step
Pretty
A spray of red on the snow
My muddled mind tries to make sense of the red
A Sherpa grabs my arm, pointing to the snow and talking excitedly
Pulling me away and calling for the doctor
Why?

Deep rasping cough
A knife in my throat
The doctor insists I return to a lower altitude
My body's not ready
I have to stop
Sleep
Try later

ACCLIMATIZING

It is imperative to acclimate oneself to the high altitude on Mount Everest, if we want to climb it. If we go up too fast, the changes in atmospheric pressure can make us sick or even kill us. The entire trekking trip will last 7 - 9 weeks. But, not all of those days will be actual climbing. Some will be allowing our bodies to acclimate to the changes of the reduced oxygen content in the air. Climbers move up and then down again; this is the acclimatization process. It is essential for ascending to high altitudes safely. Climbers need to stay down to have a rest, but it's not good to stay too long. If we don't continue with the process, we will lose the function of the acclimatization.

CHANGE

Could there be a more clear-cut metaphor for journeying through tough times than acclimatizing? Isn't that what we instinctively do? How many times have we pushed feelings aside, tried to summit before being ready, and ended up lost or dizzy or sick? And then we had to travel backwards to a spot of safety, wondering if we will ever get past the stuck point. The nature of life is change, yet the nature of human beings is to resist change. Change is painful. But

> "CHANGE IS NEVER PAINFUL. ONLY RESISTANCE TO CHANGE IS PAINFUL."
> BUDDHA

nothing is as painful as staying stuck where we don't belong. We must learn to rest, but never quit.

Human resistance to change is innate. We must choose growth over fear. Managing change can begin with some of these steps:

- Identify the ending and the loss. When we identify our loss, it just helps.

- Ask questions—gain understanding.

- Focus on what we *can* do, not what we can't do.

- Develop a perspective of opportunity...of possibilities. Step out of our current perspective and take a different look. Yes, this again...

- Open our minds to growing.

- Look for benefits—pros and cons. Benefits to the **change**, not to our loss.

In order to change (our behavior), or accept a new reality, we must want the solution more than our stagnant discomfort (due to refusing to be a part of the change). Sometimes the situation may require us to shape our own fate by action. When we are no longer able to change a situation, we are challenged to change ourselves. Nothing will ever happen without readiness to make it happen. Leverage love for the outcome, to modify behavior or replace old habits with new ones. Lasting change doesn't happen overnight; it takes practice. My husband considers himself to be a 'trans-fat." He

"THE SECRET OF CHANGE IS TO FOCUS ALL OF YOUR ENERGY, NOT ON FIGHTING THE OLD, BUT ON BUILDING THE NEW."
DAN MILLMAN

is always transitioning to be fat or to lose fat. He continues to 'practice' a healthy lifestyle, but it doesn't always stick. He has to go through the same painful process of losing weight again and again. One day, it will stick (he will want the solution—a healthy body—enough to change his pattern of behavior for good), and then he can get off the trans-fat roller coaster.

Potatoes, Eggs, and Coffee Beans (origin unknown)
Once upon a time, a daughter complained to her father that her life was miserable and she didn't know how she was going to make it. She was tired of fighting and struggling all the time. It seemed just as one problem was solved, another one soon followed. Her father, a chef, took her to the kitchen. He filled three pots with water and placed each on a high fire. Once the three pots began to boil, he placed potatoes in one, eggs in the second, and ground coffee beans in the third. He then let them sit and boil, without saying a word to his daughter. The daughter moaned and impatiently waited, wondering what he was doing. After twenty minutes, he turned off the burners. He took the potatoes out of the pot and placed them in a bowl. He pulled the eggs out and placed them in a bowl. He ladled the coffee out and placed it in a cup.

Turning to her, the dad asked, "Daughter, what do you see?" "Potatoes, eggs, and coffee," she hastily replied. "Look closer," he said, "and touch the potatoes." She did and noted that they were soft. He asked her to take an egg and break it. After pulling off the shell, she observed the hard-boiled egg. Finally, he asked her to sip the coffee. Its rich aroma brought a smile to her face. "Father, what does this mean?"

He explained that the potatoes, the eggs, and coffee beans, had each faced the same adversity – the boiling water. Yet each one reacted differently. The potato went in strong, hard, and unrelenting, but in boiling water, it became soft and weak. The egg was fragile, with the thin outer shell protecting its liquid interior until it was put in the boiling water. Then the inside of the egg became hard. However, the ground coffee beans were unique. After they were exposed to the boiling water, they changed the water and created something new.

"Which are you?" he asked his daughter. "When adversity knocks on your door, how do you respond? Are you a potato, an egg, or a coffee bean?"

In life, things happen around us, things happen to us, but the only thing that truly matters is what happens within us. Which one are you?

SELF-CARE

Self-care is the simple act of taking care of your mind, body, and spirit, during times of stress and adversity. Not an indulgence—but self-respect.

Mind
Read a book
Take a class
Journal
Learn to play an instrument
Listen to a podcast
Think positive thoughts
Body
Take a walk
Dance, exercise
Do yoga
Drink water
Eat healthy
Sleep 7-8 hours
Quit smoking
Spirit
Meditate
Talk with God
Listen to music

Explore nature
Connect with someone

Let us love ourselves more than we love our drama. Be good to ourselves, and above all, stop beating ourselves up. We are works in progress; which means we get there a little at a time, not all at once. We move forward at our own pace and on our own time table.

Other Ways to Nurture Ourselves
Watch a favorite movie
Get cozy with a book
Enjoy a bubble bath
Play with a pet
Go to a museum
Have lunch with a friend
Take a break from technology
Get a massage
Go on a hike
Start a gratitude journal
Just say NO
Binge watch your favorite TV series
Eat your favorite comfort food, guilt-free
Have quiet time
Take a nap

BEWARE OF NEGATIVE SELF-TALK

Self-talk is what we hear when we talk to ourselves internally. It is the concept of what we tell ourselves, or what we may believe about ourselves. It often gives voice to parts of us that may be critical, judgmental, doubtful, afraid, or anxious. Self-talk, or what we input into our brains, will be what the output produces. It can diminish our feelings of inherent worthiness. Everything we've ever heard has been recorded by our brains, whether we realize it or not. One statistic I read said that three-fourths of the things we hear are negative. Let's shield ourselves against letting the negative talk in. Become aware of the subtle or not-so-subtle ways we may have allowed others' defeating opinions of us find an ear within. Aggressively combat negative self-talk to maintain a positive self-image.

> "WHAT A MAN THINKS OF HIMSELF, THAT IT IS WHICH DETERMINE, OR RATHER INDICATES HIS FATE."
> HENRY DAVID THOREAU

Back Talk

*I have most of my conversations with myself at the gym. I've never been athletic. I've never been super fit. I tried sports a few times, and it didn't end well. Because of my height, I tried basketball. I made a basket for the **other** team. With my long legs, I tried hurdles and the high jump. The coach said I just wasn't coordinated enough. In my mind, there's no point in going down that road again, and I should accept that I'm no good at this stuff. But I want to be healthy. I want to eat the foods I like and still fit in a chair. I have to go to the gym. So, the conversations begin, even before I arrive. The same old reel starts to play in my mind that "this is too hard; I'm not good at this; I want to quit, so what if I'm fat? And I talk back! (not out loud — that would be weird!) I **can** do this. It's **not** too hard. I **will** be healthy.*

NAMING

Let go of constantly naming and labeling. There is no one label that truly defines us. When we change the way we talk to ourselves, we change the energy in our bodies. Change negative self-talk to positive affirmations. Recognize your emotions and feelings. "I didn't reach my sales goal, and I'm really disappointed," is different than, "I didn't reach my sales goal. I am a failure."

How can we encourage the voices in our mind to speak more positively? We all name our experiences: crisis, drama, tragedy, catastrophe. Pick a recent challenging situation. Describe it. Is there a positive name you can give it? I often call these character-building events. Same crisis, same drama, same crappy problem I have to deal with, but when I name them "character-building opportunities," it spins my attitude into reframing them as something I will grow from, something to be learned...What might you call your next upsetting experience?

WHAT'S IN A NAME?

Did you know names come with unique power? Think about it. Nothing grabs the attention of a misbehaving child more effectively than a parent calling him by his first, middle, and last names. Then follows an evolution in titles one acquires: what others call you and, most importantly, the label you identify with.

It may be positive, as in the case of baseball great, Stan Musial. (I'm a St. Louisan at heart.) He was born Stanislaw Franciszek Musial, but will forever be known as Stan the Man. Few of us achieve labels of that caliber, but most of us do hold on to names that shape our self-image. Is it positive or negative? 'Mom,' 'Grandpa,' 'Housewife,' 'Bread-winner,' 'Only-child,' 'Single-parent,' 'Flake,' 'Loser.' It's ok to be part of a category, but when we use that distinction to *conform* to that definition, it can become a problem. When we adopt others' labels of us, we see ourselves through a narrow window, often resulting in self-imposed limitations.

How do you define yourself? How do others define you? And which parts of you are lost in those definitions?

This Old Dog Knows a Few Tricks
Working from home had its challenges during the pandemic, but when Liam's company decided everyone would present a new training to the team via a virtual conference, Liam panicked. Seriously? Just a couple more years and he could retire, not be forced to figure out technology he had no interest in using. It made him mad when Brad joked on the team call about being the only member young enough to know how to do it, and the rest of the 'Grandpas' would be struggling. Just yesterday, Liam would have ignored that kind of comment, silently agreeing. But he had pride in his work and wouldn't end his career with the reputation that he 'couldn't keep up.' He got serious about tackling his lack of experience in the virtual world and practiced a few things with the other 'Grandpas.' When it was Liam's turn to present to the team, even Brad was impressed with his animated images and edited photos.

Liam discovered a fondness for the world of technology he hadn't explored because of definitions he let himself believe. Make sure the names you are letting others, and yourself, define you by aren't limiting who you really are.

BOUNDARIES

According to the Merriam Webster Dictionary, a boundary is "a point or limit that indicates where two things become different." It is where I stop and you begin. A boundary is a line or space between two people. Healthy boundaries are important to our physical and emotional health. It takes wisdom to know what we should be doing and what we shouldn't. We can't do everything. Be everything. Boundaries provide

> "DARING TO SET BOUNDARIES IS ABOUT HAVING THE COURAGE TO LOVE OURSELVES, EVEN WHEN WE RISK DISAPPOINTING OTHERS."
> BRENE' BROWN

protection. Any confusion over responsibility and ownership of our lives is a problem of boundaries. If boundaries are weak, we are vulnerable. And if boundaries are too rigid, we become closed off and disconnected. We need to find healthy boundaries. Define for ourselves what's okay and what's not.

Boundaries are a function of self-respect and self-love. They are a side effect of a healthy self-esteem. They are created by people with strong emotional health and serve to support and protect it. If we were on a true mountain trek, there would be a guide directing how far or how high we move, based on abilities, conditions, and the overarching goal of safely reaching the summit, and oh yeah, living to tell the tale. However, on our personal journeys, left to our own devices, we often push past the boundaries of what's safe and healthy to take on.

Example: Do you ever feel like you have to 'save' people close to you and help them fix their problems? Do you have to listen to the same problem or drama from someone close to you who isn't interested in using any of the problem-solving advice you have already given? Do you say yes to an event or project and later feel resentful because you really don't have the time? If you answered "yes" to any of those questions, those are times when healthy boundaries don't exist. Those situations put us at risk for becoming over-stressed and having our own health and peace of mind compromised.

Guilt Trip
"I get so sad when you and your sister don't come to see me. I don't have anyone to talk to."

"Why don't you go out more, Mom? Go up to the senior center? Call a friend."

"I'd rather be with my girls. Why don't you want to be with me? You should want to be with your mother."

"We do. We love you."

"Well, if you loved me, I would see you more. Just wait until you're my age. You have no idea how hard it is to be alone."

"Mom, I love you, and I will always be here for you when you need me. But you are responsible for your own loneliness. We can't be here as often as you would like, but we aren't the only solution to your loneliness."

There's nothing like a good guilt trip to rein us into doing something we don't want to do. I spent most of my adult life trying to fulfill my mother's need to have me close. Countless hours were spent tied up in tears, resentment, guilt, and sacrifice from my own family, while trying to fulfill a need that couldn't be filled. It was difficult to determine where my boundary of responsibility ended and where hers began.

Healthy personal boundaries are, by definition, taking responsibility for our own actions and emotions, while NOT taking responsibility for the actions or emotions of others. When, repeatedly, our boundaries are not respected, we may feel angry, irritated, guilty, exhausted, and manipulated. These emotions frequently develop into depression, resentment, and conflict. Unhealthy boundaries contribute to the loss of our self-concept and self-esteem, creating doubt in ourselves. Unhealthy boundaries can also lead us to pull away from others—isolating and suppressing our emotions.

SIGNS OF HEALTHY BOUNDARIES

- Asking for what we want or need
- Taking care of ourselves
- Saying "yes" because we want to, not out of obligation or to please others
- Behaving according to our own values and beliefs
- Feeling safe enough to express difficult emotions and have disagreements
- Feeling supported to pursue our own goals

- Being treated as an equal
- Taking responsibility for our own happiness and not feeling responsible for someone else's happiness
- Being in tune with our own feelings
- Knowing who we are, what we believe, and what we like
- Saying "No!" without guilt

Just Say No!

The most basic boundary-setting word is no. We can be good people with kind hearts and still say "No". We are in control of ourselves. Here are several ways to say "No" graciously:

- Let me think about that.
- Here's what will work for me...
- Can I get back to you?
- That doesn't work for me.
- Oh, I wish I could!
- I appreciate your asking, but that doesn't work for me.
- I know this is important, so I'm sorry that I can't help out this time.
- That isn't doable for me right now.
- Thanks, but unfortunately, this isn't going to work.
- I can help you find a solution.
- I can't do that, but here's what I can do...

- I'm going to say no for now. But I'll get back to you if something changes.
- I'm sorry, but I just don't have that to give right now.
- I can't take that on.
- I would like to help, but my plate is overflowing.

Mom, She Sounds Really Bad
Years ago, when my children were young enough to be tucked into bed, I had a friend with a lot of issues. She called often, had usually been drinking and might even be crying. As I was reading a bedtime story to my daughter, my son came in with the phone. I asked him to take a message, not wanting our bedtime routine interrupted. When he said to me, "Mom, you better talk to her. She sounds really bad." I took her call, and I was done. I finally woke up to the fact that her neediness wasn't going unnoticed by my children. She wasn't changing any of the self-destructive behaviors she was always crying about, and I had fallen into a pattern of putting her needs above my own family. I needed to just say "No!"

IT'S ALL IN MY HEAD

I can't do this
Who do I think I am?
I can do this!
I hurt
Too much
It's just too much
I'm a quitter
I'll give up
So many reasons to quit
I never follow through
Sometimes
Sometimes I do
Keep going
Hope
Remember the reasons to keep going
I can do this
Will
I will do this
Strength
I have strengths
I can do this

Ninety Percent Mental

That's not only the title of former All-Star Bob Tewksbury's book about mental strength, it's a truth that the best athletes use to push themselves to greatness. And here's the good news: we don't have to be athletes to use what they know—because each of us needs to learn how to handle pressure, overcome fear, and stay focused. Any arduous journey to the top of a mountain, or truly anywhere, is 10% physical and 90% mental. Mental strength helps us carry on when it feels like the world has turned against us.

It's an 'Inside Job'

Self-knowledge is the first requirement to develop mental strength. Without a strong sense of self, we may feel confused and off-course. Humans are born with unique strengths, interests, and values and have great capacity for growth. It's vital to identify *who* you are and *what* you value. This understanding provides insight into the 'backstory' of our reactions, habits, and triggers, which enables us to anticipate and control problematic situations.

Knowing ourselves in depth helps us recognize similar traits in others, making it easier to relate to them on their terms. Our stories are tapestries of family threads, inborn traits, childhood gifts, and a lifetime of experiences.

> "IT'S NOT THE MOUNTAIN WE CONQUER, BUT OURSELVES."
> SIR EDMUND HILLARY

Who's in My Sleeping Bag?

Who am I? Developmentally, we wrestle with "finding ourselves" as teens and young adults. We often revisit these questions in middle age. It's normal and essential to seek self-understanding. In order to accept ourselves and establish a sense of belonging, we need to understand *who* we are. A strong sense of our *who* helps us navigate life and understand the meaning of our experiences.

Here's an example: Years ago, a friend of mine had an opportunity to advance to a leadership position with her job. She let it go. Her response? "I make a better worker bee than the Queen." What?! It's good to be Queen! Society tells us everyone wants to be Queen. Wrong! Everyone does not. She completely understood who she was, her needs, and her comfort zone. This was a big lesson for me in understanding that people are uniquely driven. No way is right or wrong or better—simply different. It was a wake-up call for me to sit down and take a closer look at myself. If I could be so wrong about someone else, what was I missing in myself? Being treated like royalty has its perks, but in the world of bees, worker bees are the lifeblood of the hive. What were *my* values, strengths, and priorities? Did I truly know the real me?

Reinventing Me
I am a strong person. I don't need to be validated. I'm not defined by my partner, my job, or my bank account. So, when circumstances had me relocating across the country, I knew I could handle it. What I didn't know was how it would handle me. In recent years, I had given very little thought to who I was. Who we are evolves as life goes on. I was just me, stuck in routines and thought patterns and activities. But suddenly I had no boundaries. No restrictions. And very few obligations on which to spend my time. I could live wherever I wanted. Do whatever caught my interest. Explore new hobbies, friendships, or lifestyle. I simply had to figure out what those choices were going to be. As I mourned the distance from all things familiar, I began to enjoy the freedom of all things new.

After a lifetime in suburbia, I embraced rural living on a whim. I found that I liked waking up to the sound of a rooster from the neighboring farm and enjoyed the sound of the train whistle in the evening. That was the start. As I lived my daily life, I looked for clues to 'myself.' New people I found interesting. New hobbies I wanted to try. Buried talents and interests emerged and with them new footing for understanding myself. I'm the same me I was before, but better for knowing who I am on the inside. I admire people who have this solid self-knowledge without needing the intervention of a move. But I beg everyone to take the time to look inside themselves to discover their true self. It's the best place to live from.

> "TO KNOW THYSELF IS THE BEGINNING OF WISDOM."
> SOCRATES

MAY THE FORCE BE WITH YOU

Or not. The epic advice dispelled by Obi-Wan Kenobi works when *the force* is promoting good. But the forces in today's world are pressuring us to conform to what society dictates. More. Less. Better. Faster. Fatter. Thinner. Good. Bad. We are bombarded with messages daily. It's a challenge not to be controlled by the outside forces of family, peers, society and culture, religion, community and law, media, and gender. It's a challenge to be true to who we are. So, part of our identity is in how we react to the pressure. Social forces can guide our decisions, behaviors, and our emotional need to fit in, or to be different. Make sure the forces that you are listening to are working for your good.

Another aspect of our self-identity develops in response to relationships (and roles), we have with other people. When someone close dies, divorces us, fires us, or is the catalyst for whichever storm we have survived, our role—the way we see ourselves—is naturally altered. Maybe we've gone from spouse to widower, from co-parent to single parent, from manager to employee. Even without the storms of life, we often lose ourselves. With a strong sense of self, we remain connected to who we are (our values, desires, disappointments, hopes, etc.). We are in tune with our emotions as we continue on our journey.

Hearing Check
My friend Chris was heading out of town with her husband when he asked if there were plans to stay anywhere else besides with her parents. Chris immediately felt defensive. She was embarrassed by her family and their quirky holiday celebrations; her college boyfriend had refused to join her on breaks. When her husband asked about plans, what she heard was, "I don't care for your family, and I want this trip to be over as soon as possible." But Chris knew this was a sensitive issue of hers. She was able to listen to why her husband was asking this question: in the past, depending on how many of Chris' siblings were also visiting, they've had to take turns spending a night at the local bed and breakfast. He simply wanted to know if he needed to pack a robe to get to the shared bathroom at the B&B. A major blow-up was avoided because she knew her sensitivity to past criticisms and asked some simple questions instead of jumping to an old conclusion.

DIVE DEEP

Modern man suffers from an identity crisis. As you work to discover the real you, think about three main categories: strengths, values, and interests. Knowing our strengths is foundational to self-confidence. But, when someone asks, "What are your strengths?" we struggle to come up with a comprehensive list. To get our minds working in this direction, let's look at how researchers Christopher Peterson and Martin Seligman classify strengths.

- **Wisdom and knowledge**: creativity, curiosity, judgement, love of learning, perspective
- **Courage:** bravery, perseverance, honesty, zest
- **Humanity**: love, kindness, social intelligence
- **Justice**: teamwork, fairness, leadership

- **Temperance**: forgiveness, humility, prudence, self-regulation

- **Transcendence**: appreciation of beauty and excellence, gratitude, hope, humor, spirituality

How are *you* creative? What are *you* curious about? When do *you* interact honestly? Review the list above and contemplate how ways you live your life reflect these strengths.

Value, by definition is relative worth, merit, or importance. A person's values are what is most important to them. They are innate guides to decision making and motivators for goals. It's believed that thinking or writing about our values makes it more likely that we'll take action! What are *your* values?

> "YOUR CORE VALUES ARE THE DEEPLY HELD BELIEFS THAT AUTHENTICALLY DESCRIBE YOUR SOUL."
> JOHN C. MAXWELL

Interests include passions, hobbies, or anything that draws our attention over a sustained period of time. What are *you* curious about? What concerns *you*? Inspires *you*? Brings feelings of joy or satisfaction when involved with it? What are *your* PINS on Pinterest?

QUESTIONS TO ASK DURING AN INTERVIEW—WITH YOURSELF

Here is a perfect time to journal if you have been wanting to try that stream-of-consciousness, non-judgmental practice! (More about that below.) Savor your answers. There's only *one* you, and you are worth taking the time to know better!

- What are my dreams? What's on my bucket list?

- What have been the most meaningful events of my life?

- What are my strengths?

- Do I have goals? What are they? Short-term? Long-term?

- Am I a planner or 'go with the flow' person?

- Who matters most to me? Who's my 'go-to' when I need help? Advice? Support?

- What are my "deal-breakers" in a relationship?

- What am I ashamed of?

- Who do I need to forgive? Am I ready to do that?

- How do I relax? Have fun?

- Where might I enjoy going on vacation? What would it take to make it happen?

- Do I like details or the big picture?

- What new activities might I like to try?

- What worries me?

- What are my values? What do I believe in?

- Where do I feel safest?

- Do I make decisions based on feelings or facts?

- What or who gives me comfort?

- What am I afraid of? Afraid to do?

- What is my proudest accomplishment?

- What is my biggest failure?

- Am I a night owl or an early bird? Are there any changes I could make to arrange my life to better suit this preference?

- What do I like about my job? What do I dislike?

- What does my inner critic tell me?
- What do I do to show myself compassion and self-care?
- Am I an introvert or an extrovert? Am I energized being around others or being by myself?
- What am I passionate about?
- What is my happiest memory?
- What do my dreams tell me?
- What is my favorite book? Movie? Band? Food? Color? Animal?
- What am I grateful for?
- What do I do when I am feeling down?
- How do I know when I am stressed?
- If I had a magic wand, what would I call into my life?

This isn't an essay assignment. It's not homework. It's a path to explore who you are. Maybe you've never taken the time to stop and consider these questions. Pick a few and dive deep. Work at your own pace. Discovering, or rediscovering, these rich aspects that are uniquely *you*, is a process: think, talk, write, do. Get busy!

THE POWER OF THE PEN

I invited you to journal above and let me explain why I feel it's such a compelling strategy to help us get to know ourselves. Writing down feelings of heartache and grief is a powerful tool on the road to healing. Journaling can also soothe us in the stream of what feels good in our lives. Ask yourself: When do I feel happy? What has made me happy in the past? What made me laugh? Write about joy and love—friends and family.

Journaling freely, without an inner critic or censure is a balm for the soul and a window to our true selves. Especially for thoughts or feelings we can't fully articulate. We can write without having to explain or justify ourselves or our actions. A journal is solely written for ourselves; we don't need to worry about grammar, punctuation, how it looks, or what we write.

Through journaling, we become aware of patterns of thought, feelings, and action. Over time, we get to see how far we've come, how we've changed, and the progress of our journey. Ultimately, reading our journals helps to unlock the mysteries of our true selves!

It's Just the Way I'm Wired

Thinking about who we are, and who we aren't, is a great exercise in self-awareness. However, learning how we're wired doesn't have to only come from inner exploration. We can take in-depth personality or strength-profiling tests, found and accessed freely on the internet. Numerous 'tests' are available to lend deeper insight into our natural personalities, strengths and talents. Here is information about two that I have found to be the most illuminating and significant:

Myers-Briggs Type Indicator (MBTI)

No other personality test or matrix has been used more. One of the most universal personality tests out there, with nearly endless resources to explore, MBTI remains my favorite. Years ago, it was the subject of my final paper in graduate school. The MBTI was created in the 1940s by Isabel Briggs Myers and her mother Katharine Briggs, to interpret Carl Jung's theory of personality types to make it relevant and useful to people in daily life. They believed that one reason people have trouble communicating and working together is that they often differ in the way they 'see' the world, make decisions, and try to deal with their environment.

Understanding ourselves and others provides a unique perspective and opens up roads to communication, conflict resolution, and self-enlightenment. Knowing my Myers Briggs personality type gave me a clear idea of what drives me, and how that translated into various aspects of my life. It helped me accept my strengths and gifts and shed light on which less-evolved traits of my psyche needed development.

MBTI reveals our preferred way of doing things in four key areas:

- Directing and receiving energy: Do you focus on the outer world or on your own inner world? This is called **Extraversion (E) or Introversion (I)**.

- Taking in Information: Do you focus on the basic information you take in or do you prefer to interpret and add meaning? This is called **Sensing (S) or Intuition (N)**.

- Making decisions: Do you first look at logic and consistency or first look at the people and special circumstances? This is called **Thinking (T) or Feeling (F)**.

- Approaching the outside world: Do you decide things quickly or do you stay open to new information and options? This is called **Judging (J) or Perceiving (P)**.

Knowing our personality type gives us insight into predictable differences between individuals and helps us deal with those differences constructively. For example, a parent who worries about their "antisocial" child could understand her need for solitude after school as simply introversion after a day that requires a lot of extraversion. However, MBTI does not determine behavior. It simply helps us identify seemingly random variations in human behavior as the logical results of a few basic, observable preferences. For more details or to learn your personality type according to Myers Briggs, visit The Myers & Briggs Foundation website.

Don't forget! This is *one* of many tools to unearth self-knowledge. Each person is unique, despite common personality traits.

LEARN YOUR LOVE LANGUAGE

Dr. Gary Chapman, renowned author, speaker, and marriage counselor, wrote *The Five Love Languages: The Secret to Love that Lasts*. His conclusion after many years of marriage counseling: there are five primary ways that people express and receive love. Chapman defines them as follows:

1. *Words of Affirmation*: Actions don't always speak louder than words. Unsolicited compliments mean the world to you. Hearing the words, "I love you," are important. Hearing the reasons behind that love sends your spirits skyward. Insults can leave you shattered and are not easily forgotten.

2. *Quality Time*: In this vernacular, nothing says, "I love you," like undivided attention. "Being there" is critical, but *really* being there—with the TV off, fork and knife down, and chores and tasks on standby. Being fully present makes you feel truly special and loved. Distractions, postponed dates, or the failure to listen may be especially hurtful.

3. *Receiving Gifts*: Don't mistake this love language for materialism. The receiver of gifts thrives on the love, thoughtfulness, and effort behind the gift. The perfect gift or gesture shows that you are known, you

are cared for, and you are prized above whatever was sacrificed to bring the gift to you. A missed birthday, anniversary, or a hasty, thoughtless gift would be disastrous—so would the absence of everyday gestures.

4. *Acts of Service*: Can vacuuming the floors be an expression of love? Absolutely! Anything you do to ease the burden of responsibilities weighing on an "Acts of Service" person speaks their language. The words he or she most wants to hear: "Let me do that for you." Laziness, broken commitments, or making more work for them, tell speakers of this language their feelings don't matter.

5. *Physical Touch*: This language isn't solely about the bedroom. Hugs, pats on the back, holding hands, and thoughtful touches on the arm, shoulder, or face—are ways to show excitement, concern, care, and love. Physical presence and accessibility are crucial, while neglect or abuse can be unforgivable and destructive. NOT receiving touch in their emotional relationships may leave these people feeling isolated and unloved.

You may exhaust yourself performing acts of service, showering your partner with gifts, or hanging on every word they say. You want them to feel treasured. Yet, unbelievable as it may seem, if those expressions of love do not match up with how your loved one wants to *receive* love, they may not feel it to the depth that you intended. Tuning in to the appropriate love language will positively affect relationships with partners, parents, children, siblings, or close friends! Ask yourself: What is *my* love language? What is the love language of those I care most about? Go online; take the quiz.

Helping Out
Juan often cleaned the kitchen for his mom and dad when they were out. He'd wait anxiously for them to come home and see what he'd done. Acts of Service describes Juan's love language. Recognizing that this was how Juan shared his love with them, his parents responded in kind, which made Juan feel loved too. A hug before bed was nice, but when Dad did one of his chores over the weekend so he could get to his friend's laser tag party—well, that spoke loudly in Juan's primary love language.

A simple google search leads to a number of online tests, blogs, books, and research about these and other tools. Counselors may use a personality test or questionnaire to gain insight about us when we begin working together. Employers may administer a test during the interview process or as a form of training. The tool isn't the primary focus here—it's the end result: Knowing ourselves!

MIND OVER MATTER

Let's face it, some people are naturally more adept at survival than others. Is it based on intelligence? Personality Traits? Faith? The ability to cooperate with others? Many psychologists point to the power of positive thinking as the foundation. Survivors don't see themselves as victims but keep their mental focus on their personal strengths and why they need to prevail. This points to the importance of developing our mental strength. Strength doesn't come from what you can do. It comes from overcoming the things you think you can't do. If we look at ourselves with honesty—wanting to

"NOTHING CAN STOP THE MAN WITH THE RIGHT MENTAL ATTITUDE FROM ACHIEVING HIS GOAL; NOTHING ON EARTH CAN HELP THE MAN WITH THE WRONG MENTAL ATTITUDE."
THOMAS JEFFERSON

know the weaknesses we need to develop into resilience, there is the possibility of getting stronger. If we hide from our flaws, we are doomed to be held back by them.

WHAT ARE OUR BELIEFS ABOUT OURSELVES?

Do you struggle with recognizing your own power and passion? Your self-image? Your self-worth? Are you harboring a deep-seated belief that you aren't good enough? Smart enough? Thin enough? Successful enough? Sexy enough?

We run these thoughts through our minds so often, we believe them as truth and fact. Continuous introspection is key. We must be willing to give up who we think we *should* be, in favor of who we are. It's worthwhile to acknowledge our own self-limiting beliefs. How else can we comprehend the false wall they are erecting between our true abilities and desires? We often base our self-worth on whether we are accepted by others, rather than witnessing and appreciating our own *unique* strengths and beauty. At our core lies substance that is exclusive to each of us.

Committing to ourselves is a process that unfolds in layers. It means saying yes to the parts we love and the parts we dislike. Having compassion for ourselves allows us to embrace both the light and shadow of our personalities. As Brene' Brown said in *The Gifts of Imperfection,* "When you can let go of who you wish you were, or how you wish things to be differently, you reclaim the power of you to shine radiantly with your true and wonderful self."

We live in a culture that constantly tells us how to be more, better. As a result, we exhaust ourselves seeking value and self-worth based on outside standards. Go back to what you learned about your own values and stay true to yourself.

TRIP HAZARDS

Stumbling blocks are everywhere. Here are a few to consider:

- **Putting everyone else's needs before our own.**
When we focus on others and neglect ourselves, we
fail to recognize and value *our* needs. Frequently this
leads to feeling depleted which can result in poor
health, resentment, and depression.

Caregiving Starts with You
A stay-at-home mom with two children and a loving husband,
Rashida had the life she'd always dreamed of. Yet, she found her-
self feeling increasingly frustrated and resentful, and she couldn't
figure out why. A counselor helped her to see that her schedule
was brimming with activities for her children, but woefully
lacking any of her own. Rashida realized she was denying herself
the opportunity to recharge at the end of a long day or do some
of the activities she had enjoyed before the girls came along. Her
counselor encouraged her to practice self-care. The more she gave to
herself, the more she had to give to her family. Having a happier,
more patient mom was good for everyone.

- **Disconnecting from our thoughts and feelings.**
Too commonly, we keep ourselves distracted and
numb with alcohol, food, shopping, and electronics,
and miss important information about who we are.
How often do we reach for our phones or a snack
whenever we feel even slightly uncomfortable? We
don't allow ourselves to be curious and explore *why*
we're feeling "bad" (anxious, sad, angry, etc.), and
then we can't address the causes—part of us is afraid
to know.

Retail Therapy
Jenna had a go-to coping mechanism when stress or problems came up. She headed straight for the mall. She could lose herself in spending money on things she didn't need. But shopping was so much more fun than thinking about that big project at work or the latest fight with her mother. It instantly lifted her spirits, even if temporarily. The shopping experience provided her with positive interactions with salespeople and the hope that her new shoes would gain the approval of others, thereby elevating her flagging self-esteem. There's nothing wrong in enjoying a new purchase or the experience to find just the right outfit, but Jenna knew that she needed to look deeper into addressing her insecurities and challenging relationships.

- **Feeling ashamed and unworthy, and consequently burying parts of ourselves**. Maybe we were told: you're bad, strange, ugly, stupid, or unworthy. Or we were bullied, criticized, or teased. Perhaps we loved to sing as a kid but were told we weren't good enough to do anything with it, so we quit. Or we preferred to read while other kids played sports, but we were forced to participate anyway. We're told we have to fit a certain mold if we're to fit in, so we shift ourselves into whatever shape that looks like. After years of doing this chameleon dance, we lose track of who we truly are. Then we wonder why we are feeling irritated, frustrated, unhappy, or dissatisfied—because we haven't allowed ourselves to figure out what we honestly need or want.

13.1 What is that sticker all about?
Linda wasn't good at sports. Never had been. A grade-school teacher had called her uncoordinated. Her working parents hadn't pushed sports, so she always felt 'behind' the other kids when it came to building skills. So, she just didn't try. Why embarrass

herself? She never played ball with her kids when they were young or helped her son practice tennis. She rarely exercised and knew she wasn't the 'type' to have a gym membership. Linda was stunned when the doctor told her she was pre-diabetic, and that if she didn't find a way to introduce some cardio into her lifestyle, they would have to consider medication. All of the years that she had prided herself on keeping her weight managed with diet alone seemed wasted. To take up exercise at this stage of the game sounded stupid. She had no skill, no talent, no interest! But, the idea of diabetes scared her into action. She began to walk, tracking her progress of distance and time. She walked with friends. One young colleague was planning a trip to New Orleans to do a half-marathon. Oh, half a marathon, like 13.1 miles. Was that even a possibility within Linda's reach? She did research, came up with a training schedule, and set a goal. It was so satisfying. She encouraged others to join her. Suddenly, Linda was the friend putting together the fitness trip of a lifetime and shocking her friends with her new abilities. New Orleans was the first of many half-marathons in Linda's future, and a new world of self-confidence, influence, and healthy living opened up. Oh yeah, and there's a sticker on her car to prove it.

- **Never giving 'who am I' much thought**. We adopt roles through life, jobs, and relationships, and never deeply consider who we are (what drives us, inspires us to use our gifts, etc.), or how we have evolved. Parts of who we are will never receive the opportunity to be fulfilled if we don't figure this out. This lack of self-knowledge may lead to feeling an uneasy emptiness or an overall sense of dissatisfaction with life—even though we know we should be grateful for all of its blessings.

Undercover Mama
Susan had been married for more years than she had been single. It was all she knew. She was Blake's wife. She was Brittani's mother. She was sure there were people in her life that didn't even know her first name, and she was actually ok with that. When Blake died of a heart attack at 61, Susan didn't know how to be a single, autonomous adult without a partner. She was mired in fear. Brittani was in her first year of school (away from home), and Susan wanted her daughter to have a strong example of how to weather this tragedy. She remembered her own college days. She had been such a firecracker! Running for student government and joining her friends at protests. Would Brittani even believe that had been her mother? Had she ever told her that story of the protest march to the capital? For years, Susan had been so consumed with her role as wife and mother, she had forgotten a part of herself. She had been a force to be reckoned with! She had been a leader in her young world. That was still who she was inside, and she would have to dust off her former self and be the leader for Brittani. Nothing could erase the pain of losing Blake, but she knew she could rise above it to take care of herself and her vulnerable young daughter.

- **Not seeking professional help.** Usually therapy requires discussing and feeling unpleasant factors of our current situation or history. No wonder we avoid it. Consider, however, that research shows that verbalizing feelings has a therapeutic effect on the brain. Licensed professionals have numerous techniques and strategies to teach us how to reduce anxiety, depression, and self-defeating behaviors. Maybe we don't feel comfortable with the first therapist we see—try another one! When we click with someone, trust grows, and it's a great relief to speak with a trained, objective person who has our well-being at heart.

BENEFITS OF SELF-KNOWLEDGE

Psychology Today blogger Meg Selig identifies seven benefits of self-knowledge:

Happiness – We feel happier when we express who we are. Expressing our desires, even if only silently to ourselves will make it more likely that we'll get what we want.

Less inner conflict – When our outside actions are in accordance with our inside feelings and values, we'll experience less turmoil and ambivalence within.

Better decision making – We make better choices about everything, from small decisions like which sweater to buy, to big decisions like which life partner has the potential to last because he or she is the best fit for our known natures and personalities. We'll have meaningful guidelines to apply to life's various problems.

Self-control – We gain insight into knowing which values and goals motivate us to activate our will power to resist bad habits and which inspire us to develop good ones.

Resistance to social pressure – When grounded in our values and preferences, we're less likely to say "yes" when we want to say "no."

Tolerance and understanding of others – Awareness of our own foibles and struggles develops empathy for others.

Vitality and pleasure – Being who we truly are helps us to feel more alive, making our experience of life richer and more exciting.

Let's focus our attention on discovering who we are—on the inside. Taking the time to know ourselves may change our thoughts and change our reality.

POSITIVE STEPS TO BUILD A MENTALLY STRONGER YOU!

Too many things in life are out of our control, from traffic to weather to our boss being irritable. Instead of getting wound up and irritated at these situations, take a breath and practice accepting *what is*. Especially when issues are not life-threatening, why give our precious joy away to stew over inconveniences and minor disturbances? We cannot control situations, but we can control our reactions. Practice being positive.

> LIFE IS THICKLY SOWN WITH THORNS, AND I KNOW NO OTHER REMEDY THAN TO PASS QUICKLY THROUGH THEM. THE LONGER WE DWELL ON OUR MISFORTUNES, THE GREATER IS THEIR POWER TO HARM US."
>
> VOLTAIRE

I urge you to treat becoming aware of positive versus negative thinking as a *practice*—in order to break an energy-draining, mental habit. When life's storms are the most ferocious, we will need this cultivated reservoir of positive thinking and clear, grounded sight. If we take off on an airplane when it's raining, we learn that above the clouds, the sun is shining. Look for the positive daily. Transform your mindset to eliminate negativity.

Unfollow, delete, and remove negative feelings (or even people, when you can), from your life. Replace with a gratifying activity or a person or organization that is inspiring! Use life's frequent, natural pauses to shift perspectives. While waiting in line or at a traffic stop, contemplate: What are the *best* parts of my life? Who or what drains my life that I can let go of? Print a positive quote you love and put it on your desk or bathroom mirror. Create a positive playlist of music and listen to it while starting the day. Capitalize on the power of positivity!

GET ON THE ROAD TO RESILIENCE

Resilience is "bouncing back" or adapting from difficult experiences and/or change. Resilience is like a muscle. The more we exercise it, the stronger it becomes. Difficult experiences may be temporary, life-long, or crisis situations. Their impact on our lives depends on how we choose to view and react to them. Imagine this adverse event shifting: a week out, a month out, one or more years out. A pessimist sees difficulties as never-ending. But they will end! We will get through it. We are building resilience muscles. Tough times don't last, but tough people do.

> "THAT WHICH DOES NOT KILL US MAKES US STRONGER."
> FRIEDRICH NIETZSCHE

- For example, say we break a leg and aren't able to walk for a period of time. Resiliency means finding ways to adapt to our new situation—like excelling at physical therapy to build up strength and getting comfortable with a wheelchair or crutches—knowing that we will prevail, even if our abilities change.

- Reflect on past difficulties and what has been gained—the "silver lining." People report confidence in abilities they didn't realize they possessed or they have a deeper appreciation for life. Know that there are lessons to learn through each challenging, demanding experience.

DEVELOP A VICTORIOUS ATTITUDE

Remember that positive attitude packed in our baggage for this journey? Transform it into a *victorious* attitude. We are triumphant, conquering champions and successful on our journeys! Walk, talk, and act as though we are likely to reach the summit—or better still: that we are already there! Victory comes from a sense of achievement, of overcoming insurmountable obstacles and surviving.

When we have everything to gain and nothing to lose, remember: *we may succeed.* The journey to the summit prompts us to look forward and to replace negative thoughts with positive ones. Releasing positive energy propels us to keep going for the gold. We maintain our attitude by keeping the faith and discerning the lies we tell ourselves *about* ourselves that foster self-doubt. Rebuff them to keep a victorious attitude!

IT'S SCARY HERE

The constant wind is deafening
Insanity is near
I've got to get out of this tent
Just a short walk around camp to clear my head
I long for the cold of childhood, sledding adventures, and blue lips
That was nothing
This is true cold
Breathe
Don't go too far
Breathe
Watch for cliffs
A crevasse
A frozen body
No!
Shock
Confusion
Mental fog
It can't be
My emotions scream that it's not real
But my mind knows it is
Frozen in a half-seated position
Lost mittens
Eyes open
Hideous
Grotesque

Real
How did I get here?

EVEREST IS A SCARY PLACE

Everest is an extremely inhospitable place. Almost nothing grows or lives at the summit. The jet stream buffets the top of Everest with hurricane force winds for much of the year. Avalanches are a constant threat. Fierce storms may blow up unexpectedly, trapping or blinding climbers. Shifting glaciers can open suddenly, creating deep crevasses, often obscured by snow. Other risks to Everest climbers include lack of oxygen, frostbite and hypothermia from the extreme temperatures, thrombosis or embolisms caused by thickening of blood in response to high altitude, extreme sunburn, and broken bones from falls. Often, a combination of natural forces and human physiology produces lethal consequences for Everest mountaineers. Due to the innumerable dangers encountered, if a climber dies, it may be impossible to remove them from the mountain.

Our journeys through pain are frightening. We don't want to be here. We want to be back where life is safe, familiar. But that is not the hand fate has dealt. We have no choice. The journey was chosen for us, and it's up to us to dig deep and make it through.

Hold the vision of what you *want* to happen, not what appears to be happening. Stay with the vision. See it, share it, feel it. Focus on what you want to bring into your life rather than what might arise. Be realistic. We can't visualize ourselves back into a failed marriage or bring a lost spouse back to life. We can, however, see our summit of being okay on our own, of loving ourselves, or possibly a future with someone else.

Remember, as the saying goes: this too shall pass. All things come and go. Change is the only constant in our lives. Be open. Adapt. Know that what may appear as a mountain in front of you will soon be a molehill behind you. The one guarantee is that the more we demand, 'this should not be happening to me," the worse our suffering will become.

COURAGE

The word courage is rooted in the old French word coeur (heart), and from the Latin word for heart, cor. It comes from the ancient idea that our character and emotions come from our heart. Therefore, to have courage means acting from the heart in the face of being afraid. One of my favorite quotes from Nelson Mandela's book *Notes to the Future,* is on courage: "I learned that courage was not the absence of fear, but the triumph over it. I felt fear more times than I can remember, but I hid it behind a mask of boldness. The brave man is not he who does not feel afraid, but he who conquers that fear."

We live in a world where there is something to fear everywhere. Sometimes we think other people don't have the same fear we do. The truth is courageous people carry on in the face of fear. The fear is still there, but you can override it with action. Courage is the perseverance to keep going—no matter our mind's warnings to keep us safe. No great journey is completed without the need for courage. Tap into your heart of courage when times get scary.

> "COURAGE IS NOT THE ABSENCE OF FEAR, BUT RATHER THE ASSESSMENT THAT SOMETHING ELSE IS MORE IMPORTANT THAN FEAR."
> FRANKLIN D. ROOSEVELT

FEAR AND WORRY

Fear can intimidate us, poison us, and gnaw at our soul. Fear causes worry—over what *might* happen. Worry makes us tense and nervous. Our journeys are fraught with enough emotion!

We don't need to add more anxiety to the equation if we can avoid it. Corrie Ten Boom explained it best when she said, "Worrying is carrying tomorrow's load with today's strength—carrying two days at once. It is moving into tomorrow ahead of time. Worrying does not empty tomorrow of its sorrows, it empties today of its strength."

When worry hijacks your mind, try these tips:

- Name your fear. Define the worry as clearly as possible, in writing and out loud. Clarity is everything. Talk about it with someone you trust.

- Determine the worst. What is the absolute worst possible outcome of this situation? How serious would it be if it did happen? Arrive at a point where you have a genuine, realistic grasp of the likelihood of this fear coming to fruition.

- Be willing to have it so. Resolve to accept the worst should it occur. Approaching your worry from this calm perspective can help you identify your next best steps.

- Purposeful action. Get busy doing something about your situation. As you take action, your confidence, courage, and sense of control will return and ease your worries.

If constantly plagued with worry, pick up Dale Carnegie's' *How to Stop Worrying and Start Living*. His time-tested methods for conquering worry aren't new—but his inspirational and practical teachings ring true in a quick and easy read.

World Class Worry
I used to be a world class worrier! I would make myself sick. I would wake in the middle of the night worrying about everything from money, parents, kids, or terrorism, to adult acne and sagging

*skin. And, if I didn't have something on my mind to be worried about—well, I must have forgotten something that I **should** be worrying about! What broke my incessant cycle of worry? I lost control. During the worst storm of my life, as my whole world spun out of control, the most profound realization that I came to was that I had no control over anything, or anyone, but me. I can't change the past. I can't predict the future. I can only do what I can do in this very moment. This day. This situation. Ninety percent of the things I wasted so much energy on NEVER transpired. Ninety percent of the worst situations I have found myself in, I never imagined.*

Live in the moment. Oh, that's not to say that we shouldn't be looking to the future, making plans, and working toward goals. But we can't prevent storms—even the little ones. So, get busy living life to the fullest. Today! That doesn't leave any time for worry. It will all work out. It always does.

LOOSEN YOUR GRIP!

We can surmise that Disney's *Frozen* anthem, "Let It Go," was overwhelmingly popular because people resonate with the theme of letting go. Holding onto the fear and pain of the past only creates more pain. But sometimes letting go is the scariest part of the journey. When our life is falling apart, there's always the instinct to hold on to what we're accustomed to—even a hurtful or unhealthy situation. Hence the cliché: Better the devil you know than the devil you don't. But, in order to move forward, we will have to let go of whatever is standing in our way or causing the problem—whatever

> "GETTING OVER A PAINFUL EXPERIENCE IS MUCH LIKE CROSSING MONKEY BARS. YOU HAVE TO LET GO AT SOME POINT TO MOVE FORWARD."
> C.S. LEWIS

we are so attached to that we can't see where we're going. Whatever we know is already gone.

We may have to let go of our spouse, parent, friends, career, home, self-image, our past, dreams, stuff, or the way we handle a crisis. Relinquish control. Letting go is surrendering, releasing ways of being and things we thought we couldn't live without. And then, we have to become okay with their absence. When we consciously decide to let go, we are really taking back the reins of control for our future. When we choose to divorce, sell our house, quit a job, stop being angry—we are actively letting go. We are intentionally choosing to move in a different direction. If we don't let go, the problem we are attached to becomes an anchor, preventing movement. Hanging on is the past, letting go is the future. Letting go of what holds us down is the secret of going up. This is so fundamental that I will state it again. *Letting go of what holds us down is the secret to going up.*

Letting Go
During the years of her husband's infidelity, Tess hung on when she knew she ought to run, not walk, to get out of her marriage. When her marriage counselor suggested that maybe her marriage was over, she sabotaged her escape by leaving that counselor and looking for one who would tell her she should keep trying to make it work all because she was so scared of letting go. Years later, when she finally did, she regretted the time she spent holding on to a relationship she had already lost.

Embrace the Frigid Temps and Rocky Terrain—It's Where You Are

This is part of the process. Accept life with its pain, brokenness, and beauty. Embrace not being in control. Acceptance allows us to engage in life where we are—instead of being trapped in the day-to-day disappointment sludge of what could have been. "*Dealing* with it is the operative word. I found myself at seven years not battling it. Not struggling with it. Not suffering from it. Not breaking under the burden of it but dealing with it." Michael J. Fox referring to his Parkinson's Disease during an interview with Barbara Walters.

When we accept life as it is, we can continue on our journey to the summit. Acceptance is part of the journey of integrating our loss into the fabric of our collective experience. We have to face the loss. Yes, a daughter is an addict. Yes, the man loved stopped loving. Yes, a mother is gone forever. Yes, addiction to alcohol cost a job. Face it. Own it. It happened, and it's become part of our story. We deal with anxiety, frustration, sadness, and worry, by accepting it. When we accept the present, we can release the desire for a different past.

Our Family is Different
As a teenager, Jocelyn struggled, bitterly feeling: 'We aren't like other families.' Her father was terminally ill. He would never drive her to school, go fishing or decorate a Christmas tree with them again. After years of wishing things were different, she regrets that she hadn't given up the picture of what her family 'should have been' and instead, embraced the years that he was alive.

It's human nature to want to escape or run from suffering, but doing this doesn't help. Sometimes we learn too late that what we escaped to is worse than what we escaped from. Complete acceptance and integration is a process. It doesn't happen overnight. And, it doesn't have to be public. Everyone has a chapter they don't read out loud.

AVALANCHE!

Silence is broken by the deafening sound of thunder
Not thunder
Chunks of snow and ice are pounding around us like scrap from
a cannon
A Sherpa's hand shoves me painfully into the wall of ice
Then is violently ripped away from me
As a large chunk of ice hits the center of his back
He careens down the mountain
Dangles from his line
I am knocked from the ledge and skitter down the frozen slope
The snow is a powerful river raging down the mountain
Obliterating everything in its path
There is no holding on
There is no safety
There is no choice
I let the powerful edge of the snow river push me down and out
of its way
Where are the others?
Have they been as lucky?
I see no sign of the two Sherpas I was climbing with
But I see a rope
The Sherpa that saved me is still dangling from his line over the
ledge
I can't save both of them, but I can save this one!

AVALANCHE

An avalanche is a sudden, drastic flow of snow pouring down a mountainside. It can occur by natural triggers (for example, when fresh snow settles on old snow), or by artificial triggers, (climbers on the mountain). When an avalanche starts, a climber usually has no time to move to a safe place. It races down the mountain, and if a climber gets caught in it, they may be buried alive or pushed down for thousands of feet. Only highly qualified mountain guides with knowledge of avalanches on Mount Everest could spot the possibility of one and avoid climbing in the danger area. If this metaphorical climb were a movie, our heroine would be progressing up the mountain against all odds, only to have a climactic avalanche sweep her off course. But, using the skills honed to get her this far, she will survive, and flourish to reach the summit. It's the pinnacle of drama in the movie, and all too real for some of us on our own climbs.

DANGER ZONE

We are taught at an early age that sadness is an emotion to avoid. Yet sorrow is as much a part of life as happiness is. Carl Jung said the word happiness will lose its meaning if not balanced by sadness. If we want to grow and change, we need to feel pain, just as we need to feel alive and loved.

Though counter-intuitive, pain is a feeling to carry willingly. We only learn how strong we are, when being strong is the only choice we have. Developing the capacity to endure life's on-again, off-again suffering can only happen if we feel pain. A wise thing to do because sometimes…things get worse.

You Better Get Over Here
My friend Becky is diabetic. Type 2. She's been trying to manage it for years, through the loss of several toes, impaired vision, and kidney damage. The factory where she worked shut down. She

decided to take classes for a second career in medical records. If only she could stay healthy long enough to complete the certification. Surgery sometimes got in the way. Unhealed wounds were awkward and painful.

Becky ended up in the ER one night with a severely infected wound on the back of her leg. Admitted, they began extremely strong IV antibiotics. She became violently ill, and they tried a variety of drugs to help her. They operated on the infection. They operated again. And again. Becky had a flesh-eating bacterium on her leg that could only be stopped by surgically removing the flesh affected. Seven surgeries later, they thought they had gotten it.

Unfortunately, she was left without skin from her hip to her knee on the back of her left leg. Her life was precariously unstable. Twice a day, they rendered her near unconscious with narcotics in order to change the dressings on her wounds; and it wasn't enough medication to keep her from screaming in agony throughout the process. They rerouted a part of her bowel to a colostomy bag, to prevent infection to her exposed wounds.

How much can one person take? This storm was unrelenting. Becky clung precariously to the side of a mountain. And even with the extent of her health issues, she still has the biggest heart I've ever known. She will help every stray who crosses her path, on two or four legs.

One day she called from the hospital. "I need you to go over to my house. It's Roger." This particular "stray" had been her friend and project for seven years, living in her spare bedroom. In my opinion, he'd been taking advantage of her generosity and open door. Disabled and addicted, Roger was living in her house, supposedly paying bills for her and taking care of her pets during the months she was in the hospital. My first thought was that he trashed her house, stole her money, and was passed out drunk. What had he done?

"He's dead."

Sometimes even the most difficult journey can take a turn for the worse. This is an avalanche.

SURVIVAL

Survival strips us down to basic human instinct. Breathe in. Breathe out. Breathe in. Breathe out. Return to "Start." Take cover in our tent. Maybe we can get a shower tomorrow. Regroup. Begin anew. Adjust our summit. Call in the Sherpas for an emergency meeting. Plan a new route.

FACING OBSTACLES

A route without obstacles probably doesn't lead anywhere. Adversity is not a detour, it's part of the journey. It may alter our route, set us back, or knock us down, but it's our journey, and it's to be expected. Whatever our path, there *will* be obstacles in our way. Don't run from it. Go into it. Work with it. Explore it. Learn how to deal with it.

> "THE OBSTACLE IS THE WAY."
> RYAN HOLIDAY

Our view of the barriers to achieving our goal affects how we react. Perception of the obstacle makes a difference. Is it a challenge to overcome? Or is the world against us and we have failed? Are we flooded with fear or shame? Fear tells us to escape the situation; shame encourages us to hide. Thoughts or emotions, or both, can lead us to stop working toward our summit. They can lead us to give up. Think about the last obstacle you faced. What thoughts did you have? What emotions did you experience?

THERE'S DIVERSITY IN OUR OBSTACLES

Obstacles can be as numerous and unique as the snowflakes in the storm. If you've seen one snowflake, you've seen one snowflake. The same can be said for obstacles. You overcome one. The next one might be similar, completely new, or a vicious circle of repeated attempts to get past it. Let's consider some general categories of obstacles.

External Obstacles These are outside of our control. Formidable: the economy, natural disasters, physical limitations, or the political climate. And just as unyielding to our own individual actions: someone else. We cannot control how someone else thinks, feels, or acts. First step? *Understand* the obstacle. Is it outside of our control? Is it so big that we need to go around it? Is there is no way through it?

Accepting the Obstacle
Becky was shocked and depressed by the loss of her friend. She cried and mourned from her hospital bed—and tried to focus on her own healing. Her Sherpas cleaned the house, removed his belongings, and took over the care of her precious dogs. She eventually returned to her now lonely house and mourned some more. Her days of being the caregiver had ended drastically.

Her point of view: "I can't change it; I just have to deal with it." Becky's focus shifted to caring for herself and her own precarious health situation. She researched resources to manage financially. New friendships were created as she connected with a local church for support. Activity filled her days as she generously gave back to the many helpful contacts, old and new, that were supporting her during the storm. More obstacles would arise on her path—and she would be prepared to deal with them.

Internal Obstacles – The Type We Can Control Obstacles *within* our control can be eliminated. Time, debt, skills, mistakes. Granted, the more complicated the obstacle, the more time it will take to overcome it. So, let's use time to our advantage.

When we encounter an obstacle, we experience emotions. Take a break. Spend time comforting yourself. The idea is to not let our emotions trap us into stopping what we can do. Acclimatize to the new reality and chart a new course. Check the contingency plan. Scurry back to base camp and regroup. Determine what is controllable and what isn't. Problem solve. What obstacle are you facing at this moment? Write a list of concerns and treat each as a separate problem.

When we see small progress, we're encouraged to put forth more effort. Make the obstacle your number one priority. Focus on it every day until it's gone! Progress will fuel momentum which will propel you forward to bust through bigger obstacles. The key is to stay determined, set goals, and keep your mind focused on those goals.

> "EITHER I WILL FIND A WAY OR I WILL CREATE A WAY; BUT I WILL NOT CREATE AN EXCUSE."
> UNKNOWN

Habitual Obstacles – Getting Out of Our Own Way This might be the hardest obstacle to recognize and admit to, but sometimes the obstacle is us! We get in our own way of success.

The path to peace is littered with enough unforeseen obstacles; we don't need to add to our difficulties with denial about our own character weaknesses. It's human nature to become dependent on people, things or habits. Sometimes we need an intervention to break that addiction. We *can* live without him; we just don't *want* to. We don't want to move to a smaller house, but we can't afford to stay. We can change our lifestyle to be healthier…soon.

Most of us suffer from a feeling of inner emptiness that we try to fill up with various "substitutes." While powerful distractions, these often create additional problems, conflict, or discomfort in our lives: unhealthy relationships; numbing behaviors (like over-shopping, gambling, too much computer or tv time, too much "partying"); feelings of anger, emotional bitterness, regret, resentment, worry, suffering or troubling thoughts. We must become aware of habits of behavior that may be self-sabotaging our success. Choosing fulfillment over self-destruction takes a lot of effort, but isn't this what we need and want to do?

How do we let go of the habits and behaviors that plague us? We first have to understand this: *Letting go* is strictly an inside job. Before we can move beyond self-destructive thoughts or emotions or behaviors, we have to fully understand what is happening within us. If we don't see the obstacle or believe that it is a hindrance, we'll never get past it.

Oh Brother!
Mia was telling me about her sibling. He was the center of their parents' world. He held their attention with his handsome good looks, entertaining sense of fun, and charismatic charm—his issues, his addictions, his instability. No matter how hard Mia worked, how brightly she excelled, their focus never left the brother. His struggles consumed and defined their family, making Mia feel like there wasn't energy left for her.

They're gone now, and Mia has picked up where they left off: catering to her brother's issues, neediness, and instability. Letting him shine for others, all the while keeping the stage lit and the theatre full. She is emotionally exhausted and filled with resentment and anger. Taking care of and making excuses for her brother has been a life-long habit of Mia's. Her emotional bitterness (and a strong case of enabling), is standing in the way of her own happiness. It's time for Mia to let go of the habit of putting her brother's needs above her own.

Ask yourself: What are the self-destructive thoughts, feelings and habits that get in my way? Habits I subconsciously continue. Choices I repeatedly make? Is there an addictive quality to any of them that I haven't wanted to face? Have my family or friends called behaviors to my attention that I have resisted discussing? Is it time to let go of my defensiveness and take the leap of faith that I can make myself accountable to my own life?

Discovering the thoughts, feelings or behaviors that trip us up, and any underlying emotions that contribute to developing those obstacles, is the first step to clearing our path. It's not an exterior circumstance to be remedied, but rather an interior condition to be understood.

LOSE THE FIGHT!

If an obstacle can't be overcome and it's impossible to find an alternative to our goal, then let's celebrate that we put the effort in and did our best. Holding on keeps us fighting with life instead of learning from it. Use new insights as turning points.

- Identify what the experience taught.

- Write down everything you want to express in a letter or journal. You may never send it, but clarifying your feelings will help you come to terms with reality as it is now.

- Remember both the good and the bad of what you can't change.

- Live in your present reality. What remains to feel grateful for?

- Reward yourself for small acts of acceptance.

Take responsibility. How many times when we're angry, do we focus on what someone else did that was wrong? This essentially gives away our power! When we focus on what *we* could have done better, we will often feel empowered and less bitter. This doesn't necessarily mean we did anything wrong, or maybe we did. But accepting actions that did not support our best interests, with self-compassion, softens the critical, internal voice that may be yelling in our heads. Humans are flawed; of course, we'll misstep on our journey. But our work here is to find a way to release the pattern of negative energy and anger. Let it go.

We often believe that by changing unhappy surroundings, we will bring an end to our unhappiness. It is futile to try to change the external world. We can only change our own attitudes and viewpoints. When we change ourselves, it's as if we have changed the world. This is a discovery we can always choose!

> "IF YOU LET GO A LITTLE, YOU WILL HAVE A LITTLE HAPPINESS. IF YOU LET GO A LOT, YOU WILL HAVE A LOT OF HAPPINESS. IF YOU LET GO COMPLETELY, YOU WILL BE FREE."
> AJAHN CHAH

Letting go of limited aspects of ourselves is the same as letting go of our problems. I fought so hard to hold onto everything I'd always thought most important. Ultimately, it didn't seem to matter anymore. Insight into our problems makes them reveal the hidden hold they have on our reactions to others. Knowing what we need to do and actually doing it are two totally different things—especially when it comes to taking a step or two off of the well-worn path of old habits. But we will!

Don't Fight It

Amber had been in foster care for more years at 16 than she had been with her family. She barely remembered having one. She was unattached, unloved, unwanted. She didn't trust kindness and had a lifetime of proof that when someone was nice to you, it was because they wanted something: money for taking her in or the unpaid labor she could provide.

When Mrs. Watson kept coming back, kept reaching out, kept taking all of her crap, she cracked, a little. But she had built up a persona of anger for so long. She dressed in a way that encouraged people to keep their distance, not because she especially liked it. She didn't trust, she didn't know how. But, to let the walls drop... to be able to be herself with someone. To let go of the fight was a tempting dream. As Mrs. Watson continued to show her love, kindness, and respect, Amber slowly changed her habit of always acting angry. Hope had bloomed on her journey, and perhaps she will someday be able to trust and feel loved.

What Have You Done for Me Lately?

Let's ask ourselves: What have my obstacles done for me? Did they bolster my determination? Did they teach me a useful lesson I'll need in order to meet my goal? Did they help me identify a piece of the puzzle I'm trying to solve? Did they shine a light on anything useful or interesting or important that I might have otherwise missed? Did they help me develop creativity? Once overcome, did I feel a sense of satisfaction and pride? Try to find meaning in the challenge.

Take inspiration from stoicism, the ancient Greek philosophy of enduring pain or adversity with perseverance and resilience. Stoics focus on things they can control, let go of everything else, and turn new obstacles into opportunities to get better, stronger, tougher. As Marcus Aurelius put it nearly 2000 years ago: "The impediment to action advances action. What stands in the way becomes the way."

Famous People and Obstacles They Overcame:

Bill Gates' first business failed.
Louis Zamperini remained 'Unbroken' by his PTSD.
Ashley Judd was abused as a child.
Kristi Yamaguchi was born with club feet.
Shia LeBeouf grew up in poverty.

Mark Wahlberg was a drug addict and physically violent.
Stephen King's first novel was rejected 30 times.
Jay-Z couldn't get signed to any record labels.
Vincent Van Gogh sold only one painting in his lifetime.
Charlize Theron witnessed her mother kill her father.
Stephen Spielberg was rejected from USC, twice.

PUSHING OUR LIMITS

I like to test myself. Little challenges to see how I'm doing. Dangerous? Sometimes. But it can also be validating. I surprise myself, in good ways and bad.

Test Drive
I drove by our old house today…and completely fell apart. I had to pull over until the tears subsided and I could make it home to the sanctity of the new life I hate.

I drove by our old house today and noticed how the new owners had changed the landscaping. It looks awful. I saw an old neighbor in their yard but pretended I didn't notice them.

I drove by our old house today on my way to have dinner with old friends and neighbors. We had the BEST time! Next month they are coming to my house.

Sometimes we don't know if we are progressing unless we pass a checkpoint. Driving by my past was a relatively safe test. It might hurt—but the consequences aren't *significantly* detrimental to my healing journey. That test involved me and my own emotional state. But it's good to know one's own limits. Be careful testing yourself if consequences could involve repercussions to existing relationships or dangers to your health!

There is a
Greater Power

Sahib
Sahib
We must offer prayer
Chomolungma must find favor
Breathe in the smoke. Juniper smoke
Come, come
We ask for protection
We won't climb without permission from the gods
We must offer prayer
We believe this!
We don't go without prayer
Sahib
These are prayer flags
We put more at summit

Spirituality on the Mountain

Sherpas practice a form of Tibetan Buddhism. Understanding their religious practices helps one understand their way of life and the depth of their connection to nature. The mountains, and Mount Everest in particular, are holy places, where one comes closer to enlightenment. The Sherpas call Mount

Everest, *Chomolungma* and worship it as the "Mother God of the Earth." Rituals, symbols, and ancient practices have been adopted over time and woven into the fabric of Sherpa spiritual life.

Tibetan Buddhism emphasizes compassion and selflessness in order to reach enlightenment. Many Sherpa homes contain religious shrines at which they pray and present daily offerings. Outside, visible symbols of Buddhism dot footpaths and the landscape. Tibetan prayer flags are strung to protect mountaineering camps from harm. Inscribed with mantras and spiritual symbols, they are meant to spread blessings of compassion, love and peace, across the wind.

What talismans or symbols of protection do you keep around you? For years, I've kept a little plaque on my desk of Romans 8:31, "If God is for us, who can be against us?" My mind would want to answer that question with doubt and accusation—but reading that message would stop me. God is on my side, and He would use this mess for good.

A GREATER POWER

As human beings, we share the desire for happiness and meaning in our lives. Many people find this through faith, as do I. I believe that during the storms of life, God says, "I'm with you." It has been poignantly powerful for me to let His truth stabilize my life. It gave me the confidence I needed to face my own crises. Anxieties and fears were diminished. I did not feel alone. I also believe that God places people in my life to help me, teach me, guide me, test me, and pick me up when I have stumbled. When things continue to fall into place, even on the journey out of a storm, I know that I am on the path God has chosen for me, and I will not fail. I believe that while we may be going through difficult times, God has a purpose for our lives. There's a reason for it all, and you're going to make it safely to your summit. Faith can move mountains and doubts can create them. When hope is lost, we need faith to fall back on. Wherever one stands on religion or spirituality, having a belief in something greater than ourselves will help us on our journey.

Dr. Carl Jung, one of the world's most distinguished psychiatrists, wrote in *Modern Man in Search of a Soul*, "During the past thirty years, people from all over the civilized countries of the earth have consulted me. I have treated many hundreds of patients. Among all of my patients in the second half of life—that is to say, over 35—there has not been one whose problem in the last resort was not that of finding a religious outlook on life. It is safe to say that every one of them fell ill because he had lost that which the living religions of every age have given to their followers, and none of them has been really healed who did not regain his religious outlook."

So, what are you waiting for? As Jen Sincero says in *You are a Badass*, "Wherever you happen to stand on the God issue, let me just say that this whole improving your life thing is going to be a lot easier if you have an open mind about it." She goes on to say that whatever you call it, all of us are connected to this limitless power and aren't using but a fraction of it. If ever there was a time to tap into some extra power; this journey is the time!

RELIGION VS. SPIRITUALITY

A vast majority of people would say that they believe in a god or a power higher than themselves. Some people profess to belonging to a specific religion, while others consider themselves spiritual, without a particular dogmatic affiliation.

Religion and spirituality are terms that refer to beliefs and philosophies. They are often used in similar contexts and there is overlap between the two. I was always confused when someone would say, "I'm not religious, I'm spiritual." What's the difference? Obviously, the concepts of religion and spirituality are fundamentally connected. Two definitions that I like are:

Religion is a human invention that centers on specific rituals and a set of stories that outline a basic moral code and belief system. Religions often, but not necessarily, have a hierarchy of initiates, with those further into the inner circle leading the rituals for the general populace.

Spirituality relates to the spirit or essence of humanity. People who say they are spiritual may be working to grow and better connect with this inner force. Religious people are generally spiritual people as well, but spiritual people do not necessarily have to be religious. They may strive to attain a heightened spirituality through non-religious methods.

In her book, *The Gifts of Imperfection,* Brené Brown defines spirituality, based on her data over the last decade. "Spirituality is recognizing and celebrating that we are inextricably connected to one another by a power greater than all of us, and that our connection to that power and to one another is grounded in love and belonging. Practicing spirituality brings a sense of perspective, meaning, and purpose to our lives." Some of us call that power greater than ourselves God. Some do not. Some people celebrate their spirituality in churches, synagogues, mosques, or other houses of worship, while others find divinity in solitude, through meditation, or in nature.

It's a God Thing

As a Christian, I put my faith in Jesus. My faith grounds me, preserves me, and carries me. Where human efforts fall short, Jesus accompanies me faithfully on my journey. I was young the first time I read a poem about two sets of footprints in the sand, changing to only one set when life was the most difficult. The message was that during those painful times in life, there is only one set of footprints because Our Lord will carry us. That image has given me strength all my life.

The closer I walk with God, the clearer I see His guidance. As I began the project of this book, I picked up Sara Young's *Jesus Calling*, a book of daily devotions. This is what was written on the day I had purchased it:

> *"Rest with me awhile. You have journeyed up a steep, rugged path in recent days. The way ahead is shrouded in uncertainty. Look neither behind you nor before you. Instead, focus your attention on ME, your constant Companion. Trust that I will equip you fully for whatever awaits you on your journey. I designed time to be a protection for you. You couldn't bear to see all your life at once. Though I am unlimited by time, it is in the present moment that I meet you. Refresh yourself in my company, breathing deep draughts of my presence. The highest level of trust is to enjoy ME moment by moment. I am with you, watching over you wherever you go."*
> *Psalm 143:8, Genesis 28:15*

I have an idea to write about loss as a metaphor to a mountain climb, and the first devotional I read talks about resting with Jesus on my journey up a steep, rugged path?! This is not a coincidence. I don't believe in coincidences. I believe in direction from God. Signs that I am on the right path. I believe we are given specific, divine direction in the form of personal inspiration and experience—those internal voices that nudge us in a certain direction. Gandhi spoke freely of the need to follow the still small voices within. Ralph Waldo Emerson wrote, "None of us will ever accomplish anything excellent or commanding except when he listens to this whisper that is heard by him alone."

My spirituality—my Christian religion—helps me to lead a richer, fuller, and happier life. My sense of peace increases: in who I am, what I do, what I say, and who I spend time with. I pray for understanding. Hardships befall every living person—Christians and non-Christians alike. As a Christian, my relationship with Jesus empowers me to overcome hardship with His help. How does your spirituality help you?

Get your prayer on!
God does great things through the greatly wounded. God sees the broken as the best, and He sees the best in the broken, and He calls the wounded to be the world changers. God doesn't call the equipped. He equips the called.

KEEP THE FAITH

When my state of mind was shattered by the shock of my marriage dissolving, at first God seemed hard to reach. I felt abandoned and left in the cold. I felt unworthy of His love. Church was painful, and if I went, I likely left in tears. Life stinks when viewed from the bottom of the pit. But, like Joseph when his brothers threw him into the cistern before selling him into slavery, looking up is the only direction left. When bad things happen, it's normal to feel angry and lost, at God, at the Universe, at life.

I've been told that having anger at God speaks to having a relationship with God, that faith is a process and a journey. In my darkest, stillest moments, God could reach me. It was during the day-to-day struggle when I felt forsaken. It took time and maturity in my faith to look inside and believe that everything was unfolding as it should. Our challenge isn't only to deal with loss, but to find the blessing in the situation.

I've always tried to find meaning in my most difficult losses. Probably trying to answer the mantra in my mind: Why? Why? Why? Why don't I have grandparents? Why did my brother die? Why can't my father break his addiction? Why do I have to be the strong one? Why has my marriage ended? There's never been a lightning bolt or banner in the sky bringing me an answer. Just the ever-present whisper to help others. To share my experiences. To listen to those hurting.

I found peace and healing in listening to others. Empathizing as only someone who has been there can. Sharing things that helped—or didn't. Humbly writing this book. Loving others as I want to be loved. Trying to love as compassionately as God loves.

Can you discover the gift in what's happening in your life? Even when I was grieving the intense loss of a loved one, I thanked God for my having received and experienced the gift of that love. We don't all need to write a book, start a foundation, or build a shelter. Can you be the shoulder your grandchildren need? The strength your spouse can lean on? The keeper of memories? Or the provider of levity to keep the family putting one foot in front of the other when the map has blown away and the mountain has grown icy?

Instead of trying to avoid suffering, seek to learn and grow through it. I keep in mind that God is more interested in making my life holy than He is in making my life happy, because holiness has eternal value. From my Christian perspective, God's goal is to help us learn how to become more like Jesus Christ, and we often can do that best by drawing closer to Him when suffering and developing a stronger character in the process. Suffering will inevitably come into our lives; it's an integral part of existing. I ask God to use my suffering to accomplish good purposes in my life. I ask God to help me view hardship from the perspective of how it advances God's purposes for me. This is how I know when God is speaking to me:

- His direction agrees with Scripture.

- God usually repeats it.

- The idea comes to me while praying.

- The desire grows stronger with time.

- It involves an element of risk or faith.

Is there a way that your religion or spiritual beliefs frame suffering and growth that comforts you? Now may be the time to invest your heart and mind more deeply into your spiritual foundation. Use this moment to write your own prayer for strength and peace.

God's Arms
I was in a terrible place. Absolutely devastated. Broken. Hopeless. So overwhelmed with grief and pain, I couldn't think straight. I couldn't even form the words in my mind to pray. Pray for what? Help. Help. Help. That's all I could think. Just, 'help me.' My sobbing subsided. My breathing calmed. I sensed the grace-filled touch of the Divine on my shattered soul. It was as if I could feel the loving arms of my God enfold me in His comfort. From the depths of that sorrow I felt loved. So loved and cherished by God, that I would be okay. That He would see me through this pain and be with me always. I can only describe it as joy. Joy that I am lavished with love to this depth. I remember the day. Where I was. What was happening around me. I visit that memory and know it to be true. I've never hurt worse or felt greater joy than on that day. Thank you, God.

PRACTICE SOMETHING

Spiritual practices are at the heart and soul of the world's religions. They help us discover our deepest values, address our longing to connect with the Divine and propel us on journeys to wholeness. The very nature of a spiritual life is that it is personal. There are a variety of rich ways to deepen our relationships with the sacred and the world. Perhaps, consider opening your heart and mind to discover additional avenues to expand your spiritual connection.

Many people find comfort and develop the ability to accept life as it is, through mindful meditation. It's an exercise for controlling our attention and moving into the ever-present peaceful space within. This might be through prayer, breath and energy work, or other techniques to channel our focus. As Buddha said, 'Quiet the mind and the soul will speak." Habitually meditating, even 10-20 minutes per day, can help decrease stress and help us to understand our pain by increasing awareness of ourselves and our surroundings.

Practice implies repetition to acquire skill or proficiency. Wherever you are in faith or spirituality, keep practicing. Sherpas can help, but make sure to get a good coach, mentor, or pastor. A knowledgeable guide who has experience in particular techniques can help us see possibilities for growth that we had no clue could so enhance our spiritual lives.

The Perfection of Nature
Jake loved nature. The trees, the grass, the flowers. The rocks and land and creeks. When life got hard or confusing, he retreated to what he loved best. The outdoors. The most perfect setting with no mistakes. A window into the vastness of the universe and all it contains, from gorgeous mountains in the distance to the tiny creatures dwelling in a fallen log. The woods always gave Jake more than he was looking for. Nature and its beauty would heal and strengthen him as he breathed in the clean air and wonder of creation. As the famous naturalist John Muir said, "Earth hath no sorrow that earth cannot heal, or heaven cannot heal, for the earth as seen in the clean wilds of the mountains is about as divine as anything the heart of man can conceive!"

Bigfoot!

The "call of nature" is ever present, despite 30 below temperatures
I waited as long as I could, but it was inevitable
"It" happens, even here
Pull on as much clothing as possible
Stumble to the edge of camp
Diarrhea again
Why am I here?
Why am I putting myself through this?
Take care of business
Stumble back
Don't fall off the cliff
Almost back to my tent, I hear a crash from inside
A yell
Another yell
A clatter of pots and pans
A huge, hairy creature crawls out of my tent!
It comes toward me
Arms upraised
Stinking!
I am frozen in fear
I scream
The monster laughs
The cook, the cook boy, and a group of Sherpas, tumble out of my tent
All laughing and holding their bellies

Most of the camp was in on the jest, and everyone is left in high
spirits
The legend of the Yeti lives on
What's that?
Some of my "business" is frozen on the outside of my snow pants
Flaking off in the wind and showering my friends downwind
I chuckle to myself as I snuggle back inside my sleeping bag
"It" happens

THE LEGEND OF THE YETI

Big Foot or the Abominable Snowman is the brunt of many
Western jokesters, and maybe in a movie or two, but the
Yeti is a real character in Sherpa folklore. According to one
legend, Yetis of the past were numerous and would attack
local villages. The elders of one village decided on a plan to
eliminate them. Villagers gathered in a high alpine pasture and
everyone brought a large kettle of chang (maize beer). They
also brought weapons, such as sticks and knives and swords.
Pretending to get drunk, they began to "fight" with each other.
Towards nightfall, the villagers returned to their settlement,
leaving behind the weapons and large amounts of beer. The
Yetis had been hidden in the mountains, watching the day's
events. As soon as the villagers left, they came down to the
pasture, drank the rest of the beer, and started fighting among
themselves. Soon, most of the Yetis were dead. A few of the
less intoxicated escaped and swore revenge. However, there
were so few left that the survivors retreated to caves high in
the mountains where no one would find them. Occasionally,
they appear again. Or, do they…?

LIFE IS BETTER WHEN YOU'RE HAVING FUN

Humor can catapult a sullen spirit into a wonderfully uplifted
state of happiness. Amusement at ourselves and being able

to not take ourselves too seriously are invaluable life skills. I use humor as a defense mechanism to handle uncomfortable situations. I can crack a joke that will distract people or put them at ease. Sometimes laughter and humor are all I have. Moments of great pain are tolerable when woven together with moments of great levity. My husband is working on the much-anticipated adult version to Taro Gomi's *Everybody Poops,* which will be cleverly titled, *Everybody Gets Pooped On.*

Seinfeld
Quite by accident, my kids and I got hooked on an old sitcom, Seinfeld. At the end of the day, or on weekends when we were at loose ends or just lonely, someone would suggest we watch a little Seinfeld. Who knew? It became our group therapy. Jerry brought the everyday and mundane to the level of comic genius. There was usually something to chuckle about, or maybe an awkward scene to laugh about later. It was a simple escape. Utter relaxation and a needed break from the tension of being a family—less one. It was bonding. So much so, that we began to speak Seinfeldian and have our own private jokes that seemed to fit in whatever new situation we found ourselves. This blossomed into discovering new comedians we enjoyed and eventually a trip to New York and the Seinfeld Reality Tour.

LAUGHTER HEALS

Through humor, we can soften the worst blows life delivers. Psychology professors actually study the role of humor and stress, and how humor helps us cope. We know instinctively that being able to laugh after a trauma limits the awful effects of the traumatic event. It is impossible to experience fear, hate, or defeat when we are laughing. I'm not saying we should ignore what we are going through—but we should give ourselves the gift of respite from the pain every now and then.

Eventually, the respites get longer, and the painful times get shorter, until life makes sense again.

Take Out
After a long and grueling fight against a flesh-eating bacterium, my friend Becky was returning to the hospital to have her colostomy reversed. Panicked at being back in a hospital after having spent several months there, and having to endure another surgery, my husband jokingly said, "Well, at least you won't be brown baggin' it anymore!" Too far? Apparently not. She told that joke to every doctor, nurse, and aide that came into the room. It gave her a release from the anxiety of being there—and helped put her at ease.

Laughing in the face of disaster is a balm for dealing with intense emotions. It can restore normalcy and hope. When we laugh, we feel better. Literally. Laughter has actual short and long-term health benefits. When we laugh, we take in greater quantities of air, improve blood flow to and from our organs, and let out significant amounts of physical tension. It's also been shown to improve our immune systems.

There is a well-documented report of the author Norman Cousins' astonishing recovery from a life-threatening illness by watching comedy show reruns and Marx Brothers' movies, as well as being read humor columns. He was hospitalized in 1964 with severe pain, high fever, and near-paralysis of the legs, neck, and back, from a degenerative collagen illness. "I made the joyous discovery that 10 minutes of genuine belly laughter had an anesthetic effect and would give me at least two hours of pain-free sleep," he wrote. He felt that the drug responsible for his returning to health was: laughter. Best of all, this priceless medicine is fun, free, and easy to use.

Humor is Infectious

The sound of laughter is far more contagious than any cough, sniffle, or sneeze. More than just a respite from sadness and pain, laughter gives us the courage and strength to find new sources of meaning and hope. Even in the most difficult of times, a laugh—or even simply a smile—can transform a somber mood to one of possibility.

Instead of complaining about life's frustrations, see if you can laugh about them. Comedians exaggerate their troubles for the sake of a joke, spinning negative events with a perspective of humor. Here's a jest you might like: "What would you like people to say when they look in your casket?" One man said, "I'd like them to say I was a fine family man." A woman said, "I'd like them to say I helped people." Another responded, "I'd like them to say, Look! I think she's moving." Humor shifts our perspective, allowing us to see situations in a more realistic, less threatening light. Problems shrink to a manageable size. If a person can laugh in the face of adversity, that individual will be happy throughout life.

Laugh More, Think Less

Someone once said that a joke can be the shortest distance between two people. Difficult times put a strain on existing relationships and leave people struggling for words or connection. Humor might bridge that gap. Silliness and playful communication trigger positive feelings and foster emotional connection. Shared laughter is one of the most effective tools for keeping relationships joyful, full of vitality, and resilience. This bond can act as a strong buffer against stress, disagreements, and disappointment. For example, if you and your dad experience one hour a week laughing together, that feeling of positive energy will be present next month when you help each other get through your first of Mom's birthdays without her.

Live to laugh and laugh to live. Incorporating more humor and play into daily interactions can improve the quality of our love relationships—as well as connections with co-workers, family members, and friends. Lightness in relationships allows us to:

- **Be more spontaneous.** Humor gets us out of our heads and away from our troubles.

- **Let go of defensiveness.** Laughter helps us forget judgements, criticisms, and doubts.

- **Release inhibitions.** Fear of holding back and holding on are set aside.

- **Express our true feelings.** Deeply felt emotions are allowed to rise to the surface.

The ability to laugh, play, and have fun with others not only makes life more enjoyable but also helps us solve problems, connect with others, and be more creative. While some may be born funny, the ability to find humor can also be a learned way of thinking. People who incorporate humor and play into their daily lives find that it renews them, as well as their relationships.

I LOVE FUNNY! EASY WAYS TO ADD HUMOR TO YOUR LIFE.

- Watch a funny movie, TV show, or recorded stand-up act.

- Read a humorous blog.

- Seek out funny people.

- Share a good joke or a funny story.

- Check out your bookstore's humor section.

- Host a game night with friends.

- Play with a pet.

- Go to a "laughter yoga" class.

- Goof around with children.

- Do something silly.

- Make time for fun activities (e.g. bowling, miniature golf, karaoke).

- Buy a comic-a-day calendar.

- Look for local comedy shows and performances.

- Your local library has books filled with jokes, riddles, and funny anecdotes.

- Watch funny YouTube videos.

Smile. Smiling is the baby sister of laughter. Research shows that smiling, even for a few seconds, triggers positive emotions. It stimulates the release of neuropeptides that work toward fighting off stress and unleash the feel-good neurotransmitters serotonin, dopamine, and endorphins. Serotonin acts as a natural antidepressant, dopamine stimulates the reward centers of the brain, and endorphins are natural painkillers. Smiling also seems to reward the brains of those who see us smiling. Like laughter, smiling is contagious. When you look at someone or see something even mildly pleasing, practice smiling.

What's funny? When you hear laughter, move toward it. Sometimes humor and laughter are private, a shared joke among a small group, but usually not. More often, people are quite happy to share something funny because it gives them an opportunity to laugh again and feed off the humor you find in it. When you hear a chuckle, seek it out and ask, "What's funny?"

Be Playful. Spend time with fun, uninhibited people. Folks who laugh easily—at themselves and at life's absurdities—who routinely find the humor in everyday events. Their playful point of view and mirth are contagious. At least one of your Sherpas should be a good partner in laughter.

GBF. Good. Bad. Funny. Bring humor into conversations. Two friends and I keep in touch with weekly group emails that we call GBF. Those are the headings, and we share highlights from the week of each. This keeps us connected. It also keeps us grounded. Even when things are bad, or it's been a tough week, we *have* to think of something funny to share.

Humor, being funny, finding the ridiculous in life is a skill, like everything else. Let's laugh at ourselves; it's the easiest place to begin. It keeps us humble and keeps us from taking ourselves too seriously. Life happens to us all.

SUMMIT!

The summit is sitting before me—just waiting to be claimed
This is it
This is it
This is it?
The journey has been so long
The weather is clear, calm, warm, and quiet
The pain is forgotten
My soul responds to the spectacular view
A brief moment of Euphoria
A buried realization that "This is it."
I did it
Disbelief
Exaltation
Frozen tears and tokens of success
Disbelief
Pride
A photo
The wind has risen again and is blowing icy pellets of summit
snow into my face
Moving on
Only I would know that the summit had been the easiest part
of the journey

PUSH FOR THE SUMMIT

You've made it to the Death Zone of Everest, above 26,000 feet. The air has only 33% of the oxygen found at sea level. If you are lucky enough to have clear weather and low winds, you can make a bid for the summit. Your push would begin at midnight, with you hoping to reach it within a period of 10 - 12 hours. This half-day trek through imposing rock steps, avalanche hazards, and past 8000-foot drops, will get you to the peak—where you can spend less than half an hour before descending 10 - 12 hours before darkness sets in. The summit is the culmination of your journey. The satisfaction of overcoming the obstacles to get there. You can feel the energy. At the summit of Everest, there is no time to waste and no hot cocoa sipped.

You've reached the peak of *your* mountain, but your journey is not over. In life, they never truly are, and that one great moment of "arrival" is hard to name. But subtle changes and small advances are perceived. On this metaphorical summit, it's our chance to stop, look around, and acknowledge that "We made it!" C.S. Lewis wrote in *A Grief Observed,* "There was no sudden, striking, and emotional transition. Like the warming of a room or the coming of daylight, when you first notice them, they have already been going on for some time."

ACCEPTANCE

Acceptance in human psychology is a person's assent to the reality of a situation, without attempting to change it or protest. We must lean into the wind and accept the storm. The concept is close in meaning to acquiescence, derived from the Latin 'acquiescere' (to find rest in). Acceptance allows us to find rest in where we are, thus gaining the energy to move

> HE WHO LIVES IN HARMONY WITH HIMSELF LIVES IN HARMONY WITH THE WORLD."
> MARCUS AURELIUS

forward in life, creating a new path for ourselves. "Today, I will live in acceptance, not expectation." It allows us to engage in life on its own terms, not fighting against disappointment or regrets. It doesn't mean that everything is perfect—it means we are willing to look beyond the imperfections. "This is my life. This is who I am and how things are. I am content with the situation and know that I do not have to control it, or change it."

HUMILITY

The perspective of looking down on the world from atop the highest mountain illuminates an innate understanding of how small our place is in this devastatingly vast existence. This naturally leads to humility. How could we possibly expect to control all aspects of our life? Our human weaknesses, frailties, and vulnerabilities stare us directly in the eye. One human being out of seven billion. Humility is essential for recognizing our peace.

Our ego becomes humbled through pain. One of the greatest enigmas of human behavior is the way we convince ourselves that others are not sharing a similar experience of life. We imagine we are unique in our eccentricities or failures or longings. We try to appear as happy and well-adjusted as we believe others are, feeling shame when we stumble and fall. The truth: we are not alone. Everyone is somewhere on the journey from pain to peace.

Just One
Jamie was volunteering at the local food pantry. She started months ago when her world was altered by a virus and she had time on her hands. Helping others. That seemed right. And it kept her from falling into a funk, home alone and paralyzed by fear.

At the food pantry, Jamie worked alongside wonderful people. Many, it turned out, were not there due to the crisis, but were regular weekly volunteers. Faye, in particular, drew her attention. Sorting potatoes or talking to a young mother, Faye always listened, worked hard, or gave out hugs. Jamie had even seen Faye slip some cash to a mom to buy her daughter a 'real' birthday cake, with candles and frosting flowers. Jamie was stunned one night to see her new friend's peaceful face on the six o'clock news. Faye's husband was the CEO of the largest business in town, and his board had thrown him a 'virtual' birthday party in honor of his 65th. Who knew? Faye had the means (and probably staff), to have stayed home during the quarantine to watch movies in her home theatre. Jamie couldn't wait to see Faye and question her about what it was like to be wealthy and a 'power couple.'

Jamie felt disappointed when Faye laughed off her questions. "Oh Jamie, I'm no different than you. Just two human beings reaching out beyond ourselves to make a positive difference in the lives of others." Faye asked her, "What makes me any different from any one of these people here? Life brings joy and despair to every single one of us. Remembering that I am not special brings me the greatest joy. You know who's special, Jamie? That strong and courageous mother who works hard every day and rides a bus 45 minutes to get here with the hope of finding the ingredients to make one of her daughter's favorite dishes for her birthday. That's who's special."

Jamie found herself inspired and changed by Faye's attitude. Faye was blessed with choices but chose to live out her beliefs instead of simply talking about them. Jamie came to understand that Faye was not special due to her circumstances, only her circumstances were special. What made Faye special was that she knew no one was better than anyone else, and no one's happiness or human dignity mattered more than anyone else's. Caring, with tenderness, love, and grace, is what gives us power beyond measure.

Great Things Take Time

Life is not about living in the future or in the past. Life is about accepting the present moment. Reaching the summit took hard work, perseverance, and patience. With patience, our **potential** is greatly expanded. If our desires were fulfilled immediately, we'd miss out on the joys of anticipation and progress. Patience has not been about waiting; it's been the ability to keep a good attitude while working hard to move forward, to stay focused, trusting that the way to climb a mountain is one step at a time.

> "VALUE THAT ARRIVES IN AN INSTANT IS OFTEN GONE IN AN INSTANT. VALUE THAT TAKES TIME AND COMMITMENT TO CREATE OFTEN OUTLIVES ITS CREATOR—YOU."
> UNKNOWN

Bottom line: We deserve more than mere instant gratification.

So much of the focus of this book has been about reaching the summit. But, is this the end? Where do we go from here? Life is lived in the real world, back at normal altitudes with the hordes of humanity. As euphoric as reaching the summit has been, our trek and danger has not ended. We must descend.

THE DESCENT

Down
My joy at the summit was overshadowed
By my fear to get down
To safety
To oxygen
As I began my descent, snow started to fall
I was startled out of my exhaustion by a deafening boom
Avalanche!?
My impaired mind raced
Hindered by the slow movements of my bone-tired limbs
Another BOOM!
A thunderstorm below
Fear made breathing almost impossible
I could feel my heartbeat in my mind
My entire body was numb with cold and exhaustion
Down
Down
Fear
Panic
But even the panic was somehow numbed
Dazed
Deep physical exhaustion
This is the hardest part!
I summitted! I want to stop now
Why is there more?

Down
No margin for error
Don't think about deaths that occur on descent
No mistakes
I will not give up. I've come too far
I deserve this, for me. I will not give up
I will not die
They said this would be hard too
Down
To oxygen. To camp
Sleep

DESCENDING

As difficult as it is to scale a mountain, coming back down can be far more deadly. Many climbers who perish on Everest die while descending the upper slopes—often after having reached the "Death Zone" and summit. The high elevation and corresponding lack of oxygen impair an exhausted climber's thought processes and decisions. The brain operates in slow motion. Couple that with extreme temperatures, wind, dangerous icefalls that are more active later in the afternoon, and the risk for tragedy increases.

FORGIVENESS

You've reached your personal summit. What could be left? One of the most difficult and courageous parts of the journey is often overlooked. Forgiveness—of ourselves and others. Archbishop Desmond Tutu said, "Forgiveness is the only way to heal ourselves and to be free from the past." As he and his daughter, the Reverend Mpho Tutu explain in *The Book of Forgiving: The Fourfold Path for Healing Ourselves and Our World,* "Without forgiveness, we remain tethered to the person (or action), who harmed us. We are bound to the chains of bitterness, tied together, trapped. Until we can forgive the person who harmed us, that person will hold the keys to our happiness, that person will be our jailor. (Even if that person is our self.) When we forgive, we take back control of our own fate and our feelings. We become our own liberator."

Forgive others—whether in the past or present—not because they deserve forgiveness, but because we deserve peace of mind and to be free of corrosive anger. Forgiveness doesn't condone or excuse the action or the person. It allows those behaviors to not break our hearts. It doesn't mean we forget or make ourselves vulnerable to be hurt again. It has nothing to do with absolution. But it has everything to do with letting go of pain and transforming the burden of victimhood into the confidence of a survivor.

WHAT IS FORGIVENESS?

Psychologists define forgiveness as a conscious, deliberate decision to release resentment or vengeance toward a person or group who has harmed us. The act that hurt or offended us might remain integral to our lives, but forgiveness empowers us to recognize pain suffered without letting it define us. It creates space for healing, washing today clean so we can move on with our lives. Forgiveness is a sign of strength. Ultimately, it may lead to feelings of understanding, empathy and compassion for the one who was hurtful. Who or what do you need to forgive?

> "HOLDING ONTO ANGER IS LIKE GRASPING A HOT COAL WITH THE INTENT OF THROWING IT AT SOMEONE ELSE; YOU ARE THE ONE WHO GETS BURNED."
> BUDDHA

WHY IS IT SO DIFFICULT?

When we're hurt by someone we love and trust, those aspects of the relationship are damaged. We might feel angry, sad, or confused. Brené Brown writes in *Rising Strong: The Reckoning. The Rumble. The Revolution,* "Forgiveness is so difficult because it involves death and grief." Your love or trust may have been killed. Your expectations abandoned.

The Book of Forgiving outlines a universal fourfold path to forgiveness. This is a commitment to a process of transformation. The following are the basic steps:

- Telling your story

- Naming the hurt

- Granting forgiveness

- Renewing or releasing the relationship

As we let go of grudges, we'll no longer define our life by how we've been hurt.

Please Stop Drinking, Daddy.
David's father was an alcoholic. He drank every day. Drove drunk, worked drunk, and passed out drunk every night. As his health deteriorated, David begged his father to stop drinking. "If you don't stop, you are going to die!" And this did come to pass, when David was in his teens. Bitter and angry, David couldn't remember his father without resentment. He was ashamed of his past and held onto his dirty family secret with an iron fist.

Years later, when David had children of his own, his minister talked about forgiveness and asked the congregation to think of someone in their lives who they needed to forgive. He realized in that moment that he had never forgiven his father for being an alcoholic. As an adult, he understood that alcoholism is a disease. He released his expectations that his father had control over his drinking and was able to forgive him. He could then remember him with the love that he had been denying. He no longer felt guilty for a childhood that was scarred. It simply was part of his story that had shaped him to be himself and a better father to his own children.

HEALTH BENEFITS OF FORGIVING

Forgiveness is not just a formality, but a state of mind. And that loving, accepting mentality can lift a lot of burdens—mentally AND physically. Research tells us that happy people are more likely to forgive, but also—that forgiving others makes them happier! Fostering a forgiving heart can protect us from the negative effects of stress. When we dwell on grudges, our blood pressure spikes, our heart rate increases, and our body suffers the damage. Wayne Dyer said it best when he said, "Forgiveness is the most powerful thing that you can do for your physiology and your spirituality. Yet, it remains one of the least attractive things to us, largely because our egos rule so unequivocally. To forgive is somehow associated with saying that it is all right, that we accept the evil deed. But this is not forgiveness. Forgiveness means that you fill yourself with love and you radiate that love outward and refuse to hang onto the venom or hatred that was engendered by the behaviors that caused the wounds."

When we *can't* forgive, we might:

- Bring anger and bitterness into every relationship and new experience.

- Become so wrapped up in the past wrong that we can't enjoy the present.

- Become depressed or anxious.

- Feel that life lacks meaning or purpose, or that we're at odds with our spiritual beliefs.

- Lose valuable and enriching connectedness with others or be unable to experience a depth of intimacy with them.

True forgiveness is a challenge, especially if someone hurt us in a way that contradicted our values and morals. It's a process that takes time and energy. However, it's important to remember that holding that grudge is not going to fix anything. Let go of that burning coal and feel the delight of relinquishing mental and emotional burdens.

DON'T JUST TAKE MY WORD FOR IT

"It's one of the greatest gifts you can give yourself, to forgive. Forgive everybody." ~ Maya Angelou

"The weak can never forgive. Forgiveness is the attribute of the strong." ~ Gandhi

"We must develop and maintain the capacity to forgive. He who is devoid of the power to forgive is devoid of the power to love. There is some good in the worst of us and some evil in the best of us. When we discover this, we are less prone to hate our enemies." ~ Martin Luther King, Jr.

"The practice of forgiveness is our most important contribution to the healing of the world." ~ Marianne Williamson

I wondered if that was how forgiveness budded; not with the fanfare of epiphany, but with pain gathering its things, packing up, and slipping away unannounced in the middle of the night." ~ Khaled Hosseini (*The Kite Runner*)

"To be wronged is nothing, unless you continue to remember it." ~ Confucius

Love yourself enough to let go of the toxicity from your life and free yourself from anger, bitterness, and resentments. If you're mad, be mad. Don't hide and suppress your feelings. Let it out, but once you're done with being mad, allow forgiveness to enter your heart. Let go and love!

Back in the Real World

I am not the same
What?
The buzz of conversation is as constant as the roar of the wind
on the mountain
What?
What are these people talking about?
Problems
Issues
Pain
I see problems through new eyes
Fear cannot control me
I have survived worse
I have defied death!
I am different
I am calm. I am peaceful
These 'problems' bounce off of me as if I am wearing a shield
I feel happiness
I know joy
*I am not the same person as I was before **The Summit***
I am not the same

THE NEW YOU

The joy of the summit comes not from completing the journey we've endured, but from looking towards the peace we would never know without it. For our newfound sense of self-respect and self-confidence. For our growth and awareness that we are more interesting, joyful, braver, and more honorable. We are ready to face the world! But how?

> "WHEN YOU WALK OUT OF THE STORM, YOU WON'T BE THE SAME PERSON THAT WALKED IN. THAT'S WHAT THE STORM WAS ALL ABOUT."
> HARUKI MURAKAMI

An arduous journey through pain like the one we've traversed often has the effect of stripping life of pretense, vanity and waste. It forces us to ask basic questions about what is most important in life. Suffering can lead to a simpler life, less cluttered with nonessentials. This new perception is wonderfully clarifying. This is why many people who deal with adversity become different people. They express greater affection and appreciation for friends, show deeper concern for others, and enjoy the ordinariness of life.

Pain provides an opportunity to take inventory of our lives, to reconsider priorities, and to determine new directions. How many times does one hear advice from people in their eighties who look back over their lives and wishes they had worked less hours? They wish they had given more time to their family, friends, and worthy causes. They wish they had dared to say 'no' to pressure and competition, and cared less what other people thought. The wisest, most loving, and well-rounded people we will ever meet are likely to be those who have known misery or defeat, known the heartbreak of losing something or someone they loved, yet have found their way out of the depths of their own despair. Through ups and downs, they've gained an appreciation, a sensitivity, and understanding of life that fills them with compassion. People like this aren't born; they develop slowly over the course of time. They've reached a summit and lived to tell the tale. You are joining the ranks of these survivors.

Ask yourself: What changes do I hope to make in my life? How can I simplify responsibilities or obligations? How and with whom do I want to spend my time?

Perfectly Imperfect

Meredith wasn't sure she was looking forward to the weekend. It sounded like fun, but did she really know these women anymore, her 'perfect' little group from college? Alison had begged her to come but was she interested enough to spend the time and money to travel to this little reunion? Jennifer's death had been a shock to all of them. Yes, she would go and explore the old relationships and search for answers. Why? Why Jennifer? Why had they drifted apart over the years? Twenty-five years was a long time from frat parties and fights over the washing machine. Sure, they kept in touch over the occasional phone call or Facebook post. It seemed like their lives had turned out as expected. Perfectly. Christmas cards told an annual story, but life had simply gotten in the way of keeping up with these old friends.

Who knew it would be as if they had never been apart? The years and turns each life had taken melted away as they munched pizza and shared secrets. The beverage had morphed from beer to wine, and boyfriends were husbands, some on number two. Each of the four fell into old roles: Alison taking over and directing activities, right down to where and what they should eat; MaryBeth obsessed with clothes and not looking older; Joyce, the over-achiever, making sure Alison built time in the schedule for her daily workouts and conference calls; and Meredith, the peacemaker, the wallflower, the funny one. The same Meredith the other ladies had been happy to be around, who didn't threaten Alison's leadership, MaryBeth's beauty, or Joyce's goals. It was familiar and easy.

Together they mourned Jennifer's lost battle with cancer. As they got into the weekend, Meredith wondered at her friends' reactions to loss. They seemed unequipped, inexperienced with pain. Of course, everyone was sad. Their friend had died! But as the days unfolded, they each sought her out to speak privately about Jennifer and ultimately their own problems. Meredith had a new role: provider of strength, compassion, wisdom. She had gone from the sidelines to center, and they turned to her with new respect in their eyes.

With compassion and empathy, Meredith quietly revealed the life of losses she had kept out of the Christmas letter. Her five miscarriages before the twins were born helped soothe Joyce's heart about failing to give her husband a son. She could counsel Alison about her need to control, with her experience from a marriage with a narcissist. After her own triumph over cancer, she inspired MaryBeth with her gratitude at the privilege of growing older.

Unexpectedly, Meredith became the one to sit by. The steady one in the group suggesting something fun or a new restaurant to try. The weekend rolled by with tears and laughter and new promises to keep the connection alive. Over farewell cocktails, Alison raised her glass to make a toast. "Meredith, we've been talking about you. Joyce and MaryBeth and I don't know how we would have gotten through this weekend without you. We had no idea of the storms in your life, or if we could have weathered them as well as you have. And here you are, glowing. Perfectly comfortable with who you are. You are so beautiful. You are the only one of us who truly grew up; and Meredith, you grew into the person we all wish to be." With tears in her eyes, Meredith was overwhelmed with gratitude for these women and the events in her life that shaped her to be perfectly imperfect.

GROWTH

Throughout this journey we've tapped into inner wells of potential. Stretched past our comfort zone and taken risks we haven't felt prepared for. An important aspect of change: growth. A recent widow said, "I feel I am a different person now. And I see this change as a tribute to my husband. What significance was our life together and his death if it could leave me untouched?"

If one solely needed suffering to learn, the whole world would be wise, since everyone suffers. Our journeys through adversity exact a price, but also deliver a prize. Have you recognized it yet? Growth changes one's thoughts, reactions, and behaviors for the better. Enforced life-learning, if you will. Growth affects our beliefs, minds, philosophy, morals, values, ethics, and our politics. How we grow affects our relationships with our family and children, friends, co-workers, and jobs. It impacts our very outlook and enjoyment of life, our heart, and happiness. You've honed tools of insight, foresight, and hindsight. Take stock of your newfound wisdom! Ask yourself: In what ways have I grown? How am I different now?

Me. Me. Me.
Isabelle's friend had been so supportive, but after weeks of hearing Isabelle retell her same painful story, had asked, "When are you going to stop making this about you? I love you, but maybe the pity party needs to end." Initially hurt, Isabelle considered how she did, indeed, feel stuck in a deep, emotional hole. She had heard it a hundred times, read it in a thousand books, and finally, really HEARD what her friend was saying: This conflict. This pain. The idea that she was the only one who had suffered a storm—wasn't true. Bad things happen in everyone's life. It's not "if" they happen, but "when" they happen—so how will a person choose to react? With strength and wisdom and the assurance that they will survive? Or whining and blaming, without a plan? "Get over yourself," Isabelle said, looking in the mirror. You've been here before. You know what to do. Plan. Climb. Summit. Look around. Who's in a storm that could use a Sherpa? You've got this!

Peace

Peace isn't at the summit. It's not solely experienced in a place without noise, trouble, or hard work. Peace is within us. It's being calm in our hearts in the midst of chaos or discord. Peace is a state of balance and understanding about ourselves—and between our self and others. It took this journey, this suffering, this loss, to find it. Peace that is always available, renewable, within us. We had it all along.

Hot Cocoa
In my most peaceful moments, I imagine I have a steaming cup of hot cocoa. The chocolate is delicious. Rich and creamy, more depth of flavor than anything obtained from a drive-through. No globs, no powder—pure indulgence. The gentle warmth slides down my throat, and I can still taste the sugary bite of chocolate on my tongue. Irresistible. Luscious. Cozy. Serene. A quality of existence absent of any disturbance or agitation. Peace. Harmony. All is right in my world. I am content. I am happy.

There is work, there are goals, there are obstacles to overcome and toilets to be scrubbed. But I have no worries. I'll be ok. I can handle whatever comes my way. I savor this hot cocoa and the peace I have found. I breathe deeply. I can enjoy the beauty around me. Savor the scent of orange blossom lotion that I love so much, enjoy the feel of a warm blanket on my feet. I can slow down to appreciate the people in my day, in my life. Pray for my loved ones. My heart is full of love, and when I shower it on those around me, my soul generates more. Peace is a feeling unique to each of us. Peace is in solitude. Peace is in chaos. Peace is ours.

The day I knew peace was the day I gave up trying to figure it all out. I made peace with myself. Peace and acceptance. I treasure them because they were so hard to achieve.

HOW OTHERS HAVE DESCRIBED PEACE:

- When I am completely myself
- Times of complete surrender bring me peace
- Each time my kids make it home safely, no matter how old they are
- Holding my newborn on my chest
- Holding my husband when his father died
- Sitting next to my mom as she peeled an apple for us to share
- Communion with God
- Being surrounded by forest and bird song

How do you describe your peace?

CULTIVATING A HEART OF PEACE

In the noisy confusion of life, keep peace in your soul. It can be fleeting. Feeling gratitude for our new reality acts as an anchor for this calm: appreciation for moving from counting our burdens to counting our blessings. In the direst of circumstances, having a grateful attitude can provide a much-needed perspective that widens our experience beyond pain.

You've likely heard the advice to develop a gratitude practice from so many sources, it might produce an automatic eye-roll reflex. Take this as your permission slip to stop thinking of a gratitude practice as an annoying "I-should-do-this-then-meditate-and-eat-organic-kale" task, and start thinking of it as a mindful way to keep peace in your heart and share what's meaningful to you.

Even if we feel like we have lost many things, take a moment and acknowledge: What *do* I have? Especially the non-material treasures such as friendship, a curious mind, physical ability, or even pleasant weather. Our newfound talents and peaceful heart are gifts to be nurtured and eventually shared.

- Set aside time each day to reflect on what you are grateful for: your children, pet, a beautiful sunset, a pleasant walk, or a much-needed phone call with a sibling or best friend.

- Journal your description of peace.

- Recall the toughest points in your life, then remember that you are right here, having successfully worked through those situations and dark times. Remind yourself of how capable and strong you are with positive affirmations, such as: I have endured adversity and moved beyond it into peace.

SHARING PEACE

Let your spirit shine! Go do something for someone else. Start your day by asking, "How can I be of service?"

As Tim McGraw's song goes, "always be humble and kind". As our own problems diminish, our capacity for compassion and generosity expands. Give: Time. Treasure. Talent. Incorporate small acts of kindness and sharing peace into everyday life and notice the ripple effects. Our random words of encouragement may find themselves paid forward to someone halfway around the world trying to make it to their summit. This is how our lives become rich with *meaning*.

> "THERE IS NO WAY TO PEACE, PEACE IS THE WAY."
> GANDHI

Personal Mantras for Sharing Our Hearts of Peace

- I know myself.
- I allow myself to be imperfect.
- I forgive others and free myself.
- I strive to understand, rather than judge.
- I love fiercely.
- I radiate compassion.
- I make amends.
- I am a Good Samaritan.
- I laugh regularly. Play. Share my good humor.
- I work cheerfully.
- I give generously of my time, treasure, and talents.
- I hug freely.
- I savor enjoyable moments with family and friends.
- I cheer loudly, letting my family know I am always there for them.
- I know "It's never wrong to do the right thing." (Mark Twain)
- I pray often.

NEW STORMS - NEW SUMMITS

It may sound counter-intuitive, but one of life's greatest gifts is the fact that it is difficult. Because in dealing with life's difficulties, we build invaluable strength. We deepen our faith.

We increase our perseverance. This results in being able to successfully fulfill our deepest, most meaningful purposes.

Hopefully, tools and lessons learned on this journey have birthed understanding, wisdom, and new habits. We are not the same people as when we started. We may never want to climb Everest again, but we are stronger. New storms are to come, but we can remind ourselves that we have the strength within to reach *any* summit. When we hear the whisper, "You can't scale this mountain", the mountaineer in you can reply, "I *am* the mountain."

ACKNOWLEDGMENTS

Thank you, Tracy Hart, Editor, for your wisdom, your patience and your best energy to get Summit to be the book it was meant to be.

I am so grateful to my forever friends and family for their unwavering support, encouragement, and laughter. For reading and commenting on the manuscript, I thank: my loving husband, Curtis, who finally read a self-help book; my beautiful daughter, Erin, who is wise beyond her years; my Sherpas Linda and Angie, who read my earliest draft and declared it worthy; my mentor Fara, who never stops lifting me up; my Sherpa sisters; Diane, Phyllis and Carol for proofreading everything; my sister Carol, for her stamp of approval. And to Julie, my unofficial editor, who helped me with the final steps.

ABOUT THE AUTHOR

Cindy Paige, CSA, MBA. Senior Living Specialist. Elder loss counselor. Survivor of loss. Years of experience working closely with older adults and their families started young. Having been born to older parents, she spent her youth surrounded by the elderly and infirm. At twelve, Cindy's disabled father retired to fight life and illness for five long years. Drawn to what she knew best, Cindy turned to work in a career with seniors and their families to help them navigate the journey of loss. Loss of health. Loss of independence. Loss of the role of parent. Gradual loss from Alzheimer's.

Cindy is passionate about senior living, dementia support, advocating for seniors and anything else that might assist others on a journey she has traveled herself. She is a Certified Senior Advisor, holds an MBA from Webster University, and is a speaker and coach.

NOTES

CHAPTER 1

The Elephant Rope (Belief) – Author Unknown

Nouwen, Henri. 1932-1996. Catholic priest and author.

Kübler-Ross, Elisabeth. 1969. *On Death and Dying*. New York: The Macmillan Company.

Kübler-Ross, Elisabeth, and Kessler, David. 2014. *On Grief and Grieving: Finding the Meaning of Grief Through the Five Stages of Loss*. New York: Scribner.

CHAPTER 2

Evans, Richard Paul. 2011. *Miles to Go*. New York: Simon and Schuster.

Larsen, Reif. 2009. *The Selected Works of T. S Spivet*, London: Penguin Press HC.

Covey, Stephen. 1989. *The 7 Habits of Highly Effective People*. New York: Free Press.

Robbins, Tony. American author.

The Chicken and the Pig Fable. Author Unknown.

Ziglar, Zig. 2000. *See You at the Top: 25th Anniversary Edition*. New Orleans: Pelican.

Frankl, Viktor. 1959. *Mans Search for Meaning*. Boston: Beacon Press.

Tennyson, Alfred Lord. 1809-1892. British poet.

The Lion and the Statue Fable. *Fables of Aesop*.

CHAPTER 3

Zebian, Najwa. Author, speaker and educator.

Ziglar, Zig. 2000.

Prefontaine, Steve. 1951-1975. American runner.

"The Boxer", Simon and Garfunkel. *Bridge Over Troubled Water Album*. 1970. Label: Columbia.

CHAPTER 4

Jeff Bauman interview 0:26 / 7:40 Boston Marathon Survivor Jeff Bauman: 'Don't Isolate' In the Wake of Tragedy | Megyn Kelly TODAY, October 3, 2017.

Mayo Clinic Staff, "Friendships: Enrich your life and improve your health. Discover the connection between health and friendship, and how to promote and maintain healthy friendships," *Mayo Clinic*, August 24, 2019, https://www.mayoclinic.org/healthy-lifestyle/adult-health/in-depth/friendships/art-20044860.

CHAPTER 5

Winston Churchill. 1874-1965. British statesman.

What About Bob? 1991. Frank Oz-Laura Ziskin-Tom Schulman – Buena Vista Pictures, Inc.

Emerson, Ralph Waldo. 1803-1882. American poet.

The Hare and the Tortoise Fable, *Fables of Aesop*.

"AA Coins: What They Are and How They Help in the Recovery Journey," *The Token Shop*, November 10, 2018, https://www.thetokenshop.com/AA%20Coins%20What%20They%20Are%20and%20How%20They%20Help%20in%20the%20Recovery%20Journey.

CHAPTER 6

Buddha. 563 BC. Nepali philosopher.

Millman, Dan. 2000. "The secret of change is to focus all your energy not on fighting the old, but on building the new." *Way of the Peaceful Warrior: A Book That Changes Lives. 20*[th] *Anniversary Edition*. California: HJ Kramer/New World Library.

Potato, Eggs and Coffee Bean parable. Origin Unknown.

Thoreau, Henry David. 1817-1862. American essayist, poet and philosopher.

"Boundary." *Merriam-Webster.com Dictionary*, Merriam-Webster, https://www.merriam-webster.com/dictionary/boundary. Accessed 12 Apr. 2020.

Brown, Brene'. Researcher, author, speaker.

CHAPTER 7

Tewksbury, Bob and Miller, Scott. 2018. *Ninety Percent Mental: An All-Star Player Turned Mental Skills Coach Reveals the Hidden Game of Baseball*. New York: De Capo Press.

Hillary, Sir Edmund. New Zealand Mountaineer first confirmed to have reached the summit of Mt Everest with Tenzing Norgay in 1953.

Socrates. Greek philosopher.

Obi-Wan Kenobi. *Star Wars*, Lucasfilm, 1977.

Peterson, Christopher and Seligman, Martin. 2004. *Character Strengths and Virtues.* Oxford, UK: American Psychological Association, Oxford University Press.

Maxwell, John C. American author, speaker and pastor.

Briggs Myers, Isabel, and Myers, Peter. 1980. *Gifts Differing. Understanding Personality Types.* Mountain View, CA: Davies-Black Publishing.

"MTBI Basics". The Myers & Briggs Foundation. https://www.myersbriggs.org/my-mbti-personality-type/mbti-basics/

Chapman, Gary. 2010. *The Five Love Languages. The Secret to Love that Lasts.* Chicago: Northfield Publishing. Quiz/assessment is available at www.5lovelanguages.com.

Jefferson, Thomas. 1746 – 1826. 3rd US President.

Brown, Brene'. 2010. *The Gifts of Imperfection.* Center City, Minnesota: Hazelden Publishing.

Selig, Meg. (2016, March 9). Know Yourself. 6 Specific Ways to Know Who You Are. *Changepowe*r. https://www.psychologytoday.com/us/blog/changepower/201603/know-yourself-6-specific-ways-know-who-you-are.

Voltaire. 1694-1778. French writer.

Nietzsche, Friedrich. 1844-1990. German philosopher.

Chapter 8

Mandela, Nelson. 2012. *Notes to the Future: Words of Wisdom.* New York: Atria Books.

Roosevelt, Franklin D. 1882-1945. 32nd US President.

Ten Boom, Corrie, Sherrill, Elizabeth, and Sherrill, John. 1971. *The Hiding Place.* Ada, Michigan: Chosen Books.

Carnegie, Dale. 1990. *How to Stop Worrying and Start Living.* New York: Pocket Book/Simon and Schuster.

Disney's Frozen theme song 'Let it go' performed by Idina Menzel, written by Kristen Anderson-Lopez; Robert Lopez, 2012, Frozen. Disney/Pixar. 2014.

Lewis, C.S. 1989-1963. British writer and theologian.

Walters, Barbara. 1998. "Fox Fights Parkinson's Disease" Interview of Michael J. Fox. *20/20* ABCNEWS December 4, 1998. https://www.oocities.org/televisioncity/stage/6196/2020.html

Chapter 9

Jung, Carl. 1875-1961. Swiss psychiatrist and psychoanalyst. Founder of analytical psychology.

Holiday, Ryan. 2014. *The Obstacle Is the Way: The Timeless Art of Turning Trials into Triumph*. New York: Penguin Group.

Chah, Ajahn. 1918-1992. Thai Buddhist Monk.

Aurelius, Marcus. 121-180. Roman Emperor and Stoic philosopher.

Renee Jacques, "Sixteen Wildly Successful People Who Overcame Huge Obstacles to Get to There," *Huffpost,* September 25, 2013, updated December 6, 2017, https://www.huffpost.com/entry/successful-people-obstacles_n_3964459.

Evan Andrews, "Eight things you may not know about Louis Zamperini," *History*, December 17, 2014, updated August 29, 2018, https://www.history.com/news/8-things-you-may-not-know-about-louis-zamperini.

Stephanie Nalasco, "Ashley Judd speaks about being molested as a child: I was in so much pain," *Fox News*, November 10, 2017, https://www.foxnews.com/entertainment/ashley-judd-speaks-about-being-molested-as-a-child-i-was-in-so-much-pain

"Celebrities to Overcome Clubfoot," *Clifton Foot and Ankle Center Blog,* June 2, 2016, https://cliftonfootandankle.com/2016/06/celebrities-to-overcome-clubfoot/

Nama Winston, "At 10 Shia LeBeouf witnessed his mother's rape. Years later he would publicly melt down," *MSN Entertainment,* November 9, 2019, https://www.msn.com/en-nz/entertainment/celebrity/at-10-shia-labeouf-witnessed-his-mothers-rape-years-later-he-would-publicly-meltdown/ar-AAH6q6u

Daven Hiskey, "Mark Wahlberg was a drug dealer and was charged with attempted murder before forming Marky Mark and the Funky Bunch," *Today I Found Out,* January 26, 2012, http://www.todayifoundout.com/index.php/2012/01/mark-wahlberg-was-a-drug-dealer-and-was-charged-with-attempted-murder-before-forming-marky-mark-and-the-funky-bunch/

Jacques, "Sixteen".

CHAPTER 10

Jung, Carl. 1933. *Modern Man in Search of a Soul*. New York: Houghton Mifflin Harcourt.

Sincero, Jen. 2013. *You Are A Badass: How to Stop Doubting Your Greatness and Start Living an Awesome Life*. Philadelphia: Running Press/Perseus.

Brown, Brene'. 2010.

Young, Sarah. 2004. *Jesus Calling: Enjoying Peace in His Presence*. New York: Harper Collins Christian publishing.

Emerson, Ralph Waldo. 1803-1882. American philosopher and poet.

Muir, John. 1838-1914. Modern environmentalist.

CHAPTER 11

Gomi, Taro. 1993, originally in 1977. *Everybody Poops*. LaJolla, California: Kane/Miller Book Publishing.

Seinfeld. American sitcom on NBC that ran 9 seasons from 1989 to 1998. Created by Larry David and Jerry Seinfeld.

Don Colburn, "Still Laughing" *Washington Post*, October 21, 1986.

CHAPTER 12

Lewis, C. S. 1961. *A Grief Observed*. New York: Harper Collins.

Aurelius, Marcus.

CHAPTER 13

Tutu, Desmond and Tutu, Mpho. 2014. *The Book of Forgiving: The Fourfold Path for Healing Ourselves and Our World*. New York: Harper Collins.

Buddha.

Brown, Brene'. 2015. *Rising Strong: The Reckoning. The Rumble. The Revolution*. New York: Spiegel and Grau.

Tuto, Desmond. 2014.

Dyer, Wayne W. 1997. *Manifest Your Destiny: Nine Spiritual Principles for Getting Everything You Want*. New York: Harper Collins.

Angelou, Maya.

Gandhi, Mohandas Karamchand. 1869-1948. Non-violent political ethicist for India's independence.

King, Jr., Martin Luther. 1929-1968. American Minister and activist.

Williamson, Marianne. American author, and activist.

Hosseini, Khaled. 2004. *The Kite Runner*. New York: Riverhead Books.

Confucius. 551 BC-479 BC. Chinese philosopher.

CHAPTER 14

Murakami, Haruki. Japanese author.

"Humble and Kind", Tim McGraw, *Damn Country Music Album*, 2016, Label: Big Machine.

Gandhi.

CPSIA information can be obtained
at www.ICGtesting.com
Printed in the USA
BVHW060902210820
586985BV00010B/269